POURING IN

Tipping the Scales in Favor of a Personal,
Passionate, and Permanent Faith in Your Kids

KIM KURTZ

NASHVILLE

NEW YORK • LONDON • MELBOURNE • VANCOUVER

Pouring In

Tipping the Scales in Favor of a Personal, Passionate, and Permanent Faith in Your Kids

Published in New York, New York, by Morgan James Publishing. Morgan James is a trademark of Morgan James, LLC. www.MorganJamesPublishing.com

The Morgan James Speakers Group can bring authors to your live event. For more information or to book an event visit The Morgan James Speakers Group at www.TheMorganJamesSpeakersGroup.com.

Unless otherwise noted, Scripture is taken from the Holy Bible, New International Version®, NIV® Copyright ©1973, 1978, 1984, 2011 by Biblica, Inc.® Used by permission. All rights reserved worldwide.

The New American Standard Bible® (NASB), Copyright © 1960, 1962, 1963, 1968, 1971, 1972, 1973, 1975, 1977, 1995 by The Lockman Foundation. All Rights Reserved. The Holy Bible, English Standard Version® (ESV®) Copyright © 2001 by Crossway, a publishing ministry of Good News Publishers.

Scripture quotations marked HCSB®, are taken from the Holman Christian Standard Bible®, Copyright © 1999, 2000, 2002, 2003, 2009 by Holman Bible Publishers. Used by permission. HCSB® is a federally registered trademark of Holman Bible Publishers All rights reserved. Scripture quotations marked KVJ are taken from the King James Version of the Bible. (Public Domain). Scripture quotations marked MSG are taken from THE MESSAGE, Copyright © 1993, 1994, 1995, 1996, 2000, 2001, 2002 by Eugene H. Peterson. Used by permission of NavPress. All rights reserved. Represented by Tyndale House Publishers, Inc.

ISBN 9781683507208 paperback
ISBN 9781683507215 eBook
Library of Congress Control Number: 2017912612

Cover Design by:
Megan Whitney
megan@creativeninjadesigns.com

Interior Design by:
Chris Treccani
www.3dogcreative.net

In an effort to support local communities, raise awareness and funds, Morgan James Publishing donates a percentage of all book sales for the life of each book to Habitat for Humanity Peninsula and Greater Williamsburg.

Get involved today! Visit
www.MorganJamesBuilds.com

Advance Praise

Pouring In

For Emily and Jessica,
my joy and delight

Table of Contents

Acknowledgements

I am blessed beyond words. In addition to gratitude for my awesome God who never left my side through the process of writing this book, I have so many people to thank.

First and foremost, I have to thank my husband for being my cheerleader, best friend, and partner in life for the past twenty-one years. Without his encouragement and gentle nudge foreword, I might never have stepped out in faith to write this book. And to my girls, Emily and Jessica, who are my joy and delight, thank you for the last seventeen years. We have lived, laughed, loved and learned together. It has been priceless.

Without the support of Godly women in my life, I would not have believed in myself. Thanks to my launch team and mentors, Deb Lawson, who has been my mentor for thirty years, Rosalie Hetzner, and Joanne Melvin. And thanks to the many Godly men and women in the trenches of parenting with me that have taught me so much.

A huge thanks to Lynn Crandall, my editor, writing mentor, and mother-in-law, who believed in me and my writing, and gave so generously and freely to support this book.

For Scott Metz, who probably doesn't remember writing it, but whose encouraging email meant more to me than he will ever know. Sometimes it only takes one or two key people who believe in you.

Thanks to my amazing brother, Greg Schrock, who contributed to the apologetics chapter, and who inspired me to love the Lord with all of my heart, soul, *and* mind. He has always been the *best* big brother.

A special thanks to the wonderful team at Morgan James including, David Hancock, Terry Whalin, Jim Howard, and Tiffany Gibson. I am so grateful.

Introduction

Tipping the Scales in Favor of Faith

Nothing can make you feel more inadequate in this life than being a parent. Nothing can magnify your flaws quite like having children. And nothing can heighten your awareness of how little control you actually have beyond passing on your superb genes, like creating another human being.

I often wonder why God refines us in front of our children. I wonder why we can't have it all together before we have kids. I wonder a lot of things in parenting. Why, why, why, God? Then I remember, oh yeah, I'm not running this show. I need to stop asking why and trust my Abba, Father.

I feel the pain of watching my kids as they grow up and "do" life on their own. They inevitably run the train off the tracks, head into brick walls, and otherwise barrel toward disaster from time to time. Watching your child get that emotional "goose egg" after a painful failure is crushing. It's a taste of what God must go through as He parents us.

I imagine the movie, *Titanic*. My daughter, as the captain, is cheerfully on her way across the ocean. Couples are falling in love and kids are playing on the decks below. Beautiful people and beautiful music travel from all corners of the ship. She is blissfully unaware of the iceberg ahead.

I hear myself screaming, "No, don't fire the last engines! Don't speed up! Iceberg ahead, iceberg ahead!"

Sometimes our kids avoid the iceberg, and sometimes they don't. Sometimes they hit a small bump in the road, and sometimes they sink the ship.

Looking back, I remember the sweetness of it all. Starting a family is magical. When that tiny baby with her intoxicating baby smell is put in your arms, a family is born. Just like that. What could be better?

I also remember the fatigue, I remember the sleepless nights, and I remember the endless energy my girls seemed to have when they were little.

My oldest was like the energizer bunny. She would go full throttle until falling over, dead asleep at night. And off to dreamland she went, behind those sweet eyelids. A freight train could have whizzed by her head and she would not have awoken.

Families are a gift from God and children are precious. Nothing is quite like being a parent.

If you are in the throes of parenting young children, hang in there. It's a wonderful, yet exhausting time. If you are further along and have teenagers, you know that it keeps getting harder.

Young and Clueless

As I think back to the time when my girls were little, I am flooded with warm memories and deep regrets.

I love my daughters. Aside from my husband, there are no other human beings I love more. My oldest daughter, Emily, made me a mom seventeen years ago (I guess my husband and I had something to do with it too!). It was love at first sight. Then two years later my youngest, Jessica, was born, and my fate was sealed. I would never be the same. I was hopelessly, helplessly in love.

Can you relate? I'm sure if you have kids, your story is similar. There is nothing you wouldn't do for your kids. Becoming a parent changes your perspective on everything. Your life is no longer about you, it's about *them*.

I was twenty-seven and clueless when I had my firstborn. I was actually amazed the staff at the hospital let me leave with my daughter. *"How can they let ME walk out of here with a baby?"* I thought. *"Are they crazy? What did I know?"*

Through the years, my husband and I fumbled around going this way and that, doing the best we could as young parents. We were tossed to and fro by well-intentioned advice and made many mistakes.

We were typical American parents. Purposefully or not, we mirrored things in our parenting that we observed from our parents, the media, the culture, our community, the Internet, and our church. We felt these were a sufficient group of resources.

But were they sufficient? Did they point us in the right direction?

I can tell you what my husband and I, and the affluent community where we lived, were valuing in regards to raising our children as young parents.

- *Our kids' self-esteem is so important, they must never feel bad*
- *Education is most important in our kids' lives*
- *We must always say 'yes' to our kids to produce a positive environment*
- *Kids' happiness should be the focus of parenting*
- *We need to teach our kids to love themselves*
- *Our kids should have everything they want*

You might get lucky and raise a good kid with this set of values. He or she might do well in school and seem well adjusted and happy. Or, he or she may end up entitled, self-centered, or at the very least, worldly.

"Between sixty-nine percent and ninety-four percent of their (churched) young people are leaving the traditional church after high school…and very few are returning."[1]

–Josh McDowell, *The Last Christian Generation*

Is there no manual for parenting? Well, there is and there isn't. Among the many books on Christian parenting, only one is essential. The Bible is the best parenting book there is, because it was written by the first parent that ever was. It sounds like a cliché, but it is absolutely true. It doesn't contain every possible question or scenario we might encounter in parenting. But, is it sufficient? *You betcha!*

Why?

Because the key to being a good parent is primarily determined by *who* you are, not *what* you do.

The key to being a good parent is primarily determined by who you are, not what you do.

According to Dr. Kara Powell and Dr. Chap Clark in their book, *Sticky Faith,* "It's who you are that shapes your kids. In fact, it's challenging to point to a Sticky Faith factor that is more significant than you."[2]

The "Good People" Syndrome

God wasn't number one for most of my marriage. If you would have asked me and my husband, we would have said that He was. But He wasn't. We were very much living the American Dream—the American Dream minus the blissfully happy part, that is.

We were raising our girls to be good people because *we* were good people. Wasn't that what we were supposed to be doing? Wasn't that enough?

We were raising our girls to be **good** people because **we** were good people. Wasn't that what we were supposed to be doing? Wasn't that enough?

We taught them to say please and thank you. We taught them to be nice and polite and do what they're told. We took them to church on Sundays to learn about God. We taught them the importance of a good education. We taught them how to fit in and be successful in American culture.

When my kids became teenagers, I started to think about what I really wanted them to be when they left our house.

- ✓ *happy?*
- ✓ *confident?*
- ✓ *intelligent?*
- ✓ *driven?*

To a certain degree, yes, those things are useful. But, they are secondary values. As I pondered these things I began to question the values on which I had been so focused.

I realized that if we want our kids to have a lasting faith and a heart for God, then we need to shoot for more than raising our kids to be *good people*.

Eternity Focused

When Jessica was about nine, she was holding our cat, Essie. Essie was squirming in her arms, and quietly let out a warning growl. I was cleaning the kitchen while listening to a podcast so I was only mildly paying attention to what was going on.

She has an attitude problem. Not my daughter, the cat. Essie can look at you from across the room and you know what she is thinking—I am going to kill you in your sleep! She's a grumpy old cat. And our very existence annoys her.

I could tell that Essie's patience was running thin.

"You'd better put her down," I said. "She's gonna scratch you!" Essie let out another soft growl. Jessica ignored my warning and continued kissing her and messing with her face.

"I'm serious, she's gonna blow!" I pleaded one last time.

Then the last growl ramped up. *Three strikes you're out!* All the muscles in Essie's body tensed and her front paws and legs began to flail violently. The next five seconds were a mess of fur, claws, and growls. Essie swiped at Jessica's chest and face as her body twisted to get free. Jessica screamed in pain as Essie freed herself and leapt out of her arms landing squarely in the dog's water bowl.

Jessica stood there with tears in her eyes, blood on her face, chest and arms, and dog slobber water soaking her clothes. It was a sad and pathetic sight. Other than a trail of water on the floor through the foyer, no trace of Essie could be found. But she had left her mark.

As I went to comfort Jessica, I wanted to say, "I told you that was going to happen!" But the words were unnecessary. So I hugged her tight, wiped her tears, and cleaned her up.

Teaching our kids to think beyond the present moment, whether it's five seconds into the future, five months or five years, is a difficult task. Kids tend to focus on the here and now. They live in the moment.

As followers of Christ, however, we live for *eternity*. We live for our glorious future in Heaven.

Part of our job as parents is to change the mindset of our kids to an eternal mindset. We encourage a Biblical attitude of focusing on eternity. This means that we must be focused on eternity as well and not be wrapped up in the things of this world. Disciples of Christ are *eternity*-focused, not *culture*-focused.

Human beings are eternal, not finite. Our souls live on after our bodies die. Heaven and Hell are real and we all will end up in one or the other someday. This earth will be gone at some point, so we must set our minds on eternity.

Set your minds on things above, not on earthly things.
Colossians 3:2

We must teach our children to think in terms of whether things are temporary and will pass away, or are eternal and will endure. Focusing on the eternal tends to separate easily what is and what is not important in this life.

Our children's eternal future is the reason passing on our faith is so important.

Beth Moore wrote this eloquently in her Bible study, *Entrusted, A Study of 2 Timothy.*

> What happens now matters then…Every present moment has future implications. This is not about your past. Not just about your present. This is about your future…Because what happens now matters then.[3]

Now I realize that I want to raise my kids to be disciples of Christ more than anything else (we will talk about what this means in Chapter 9). I want them to leave my house with the Great Commission front and center in their lives, and their eternal future on their minds.

The Sacrifice of Parenting

My husband once told me about a boss he was working for who was very wealthy. When his kids were old enough to drive, he gave them each a brand new car and said. "Here, go do what you do." In other words, he was tired of driving them around everywhere.

I'm sure that he wasn't quite so callous when he said it. I have two teenagers and understand the frustration of feeling like their personal driver. However, it seems that he was saying, "I am done. You're an adult now. Go do your thing."

It is tempting to back off parenting when our kids become teenagers or when they start driving. However, adolescence is a crucial time in their development. They desperately need teaching and coaching at this formative stage of life.

One of the few nuggets of information that I retained from business college was the concept of *opportunity cost.* According to Investopedia, *opportunity cost* refers to a benefit that a person could have received, but gave up, to take another course of action.

When making decisions concerning our time and money we must consider the opportunity cost. Most of us do this in the decisions we make every day. If I choose to do A then I can't do B.

The concept of opportunity cost can be seen in parenting as well. Just as there is a cost to following Christ, having kids also costs us something.

When parents sacrifice for their kids, they feel valued. When parents don't sacrifice for their kids, they feel unimportant.

If we are unwilling to sacrifice for our children, they will likely suffer the consequences. Whether it is parents who are focused on their own lives and dreams, or parents who are unwilling to do whatever it takes for the wellbeing of their kids, if kids don't feel loved and cherished and taken care of by their parents, they may wonder what's wrong with them. And they likely will look for love and acceptance elsewhere.

If we, as parents, are not feeling the pain of sacrifice in some way, then it's possible our kids are.

What are we giving up to be a parent?

Five Life Questions

Parenting is an awesome responsibility; awesome in the fact that it is joyful and rewarding. And, awesome in the fact that it is an enormous undertaking. It is beautiful, breath-taking, frightening, intimidating, overwhelming, terrifying and wonderful all at the same time. What can I say, it's awesome.

My daughters are fifteen and seventeen. Finally, they are leaving the house wearing clean clothes that match. They no longer get knots in their hair. And, for the most part, they shower and wear clean underwear every day. *Ahhh,* the sweet, clean, smell of success!

Like many parents of teenagers, I am tempted to pat myself on the back. And, like Nanny McPhee, the magical nanny from the movie who leaves when the children are properly trained and no longer need her, I am tempted to walk off into the sunset satisfied with a job well done.

However, I have to remind myself that it isn't over until the fat lady sings! And she isn't singing until my kids graduate from high school and leave my home.

Much of our kids' character and direction in life is forming during their teenage years and into their twenties. As Christian parents, we mustn't lose focus or parent on autopilot when our kids become teenagers.

Our kids hit a fork in the road during adolescence. And the critical decisions they make at this juncture will determine the trajectory of their life and their faith. They are beginning to ask themselves the five life questions.

1. They will ask questions of *IDENTITY.* Who am I?
   - *Am I a beauty queen?*
   - *Am I an athlete?*
   - *Am I a nerd?*
   - *Am I worthless?*
   - *Am I religious?*
   - *Am I a child of God?*

Teenagers are questioning their identity now more than ever. And in more ways than ever before.

They have to decide whether they will be the criminal, the athlete, the basketcase, the princess, or the brain; and, what college to go to and what they want to be when they grow up. But also, our kids are faced with questions like, *what gender do I identify with?* and *what is my sexual orientation?*

The questions young people are facing today are confusing at best and dangerous at worst. If they don't have guidance from their parents when answering these questions, they are likely to be overwhelmed by the lies of the world.

2. They will ask questions of *PRIORITY*. Who will I live for?
    *   *Will I live for myself?*
    *   *Will I live for everyone around me?*
    *   *Will I live for the person I love?*
    *   *Will I live for God?*

Kids will naturally answer the question, "who will I live for?" with a resounding "Me, of course!"

In a culture obsessed with self-esteem, we are told we should focus on ourselves. We should love ourselves. Because…*you're worth it!*

How our kids answer the question of priority will determine the relational aspect of their future. Will they grow up to be in abusive or codependent relationships? Will they be people pleasers? Will they be all about themselves?

Their answer will also determine who will be at the center of their lives and who will be steering the ship.

It is up to Christian parents to model a life lived for God.

3. They will ask questions about *REALITY.* What is truth?
    *   *Is there one truth? Or,…*
    *   *Does everyone have their own truth?*
    *   *Which religion is true?*
    *   *Is the Bible true?*
    *   *Is God true?*

Truth is what grounds us; morally and physically. Truth is what keeps us from floating around in space—the truth of gravity.

Establishing that truth is not relative but absolute is essential to passing on the faith to our kids. Without truth, everything else flies out the window. We will talk more about truth in Chapter 14.

4. They will ask questions about *CONTENTMENT*. Where will I find peace?
   - *In relationships?*
   - *In substances or things?*
   - *In achievements or successes?*
   - *In God?*

As I am writing this, we are just coming out of the holiday season. And the phrase, "peace on earth," is still fresh on my mind. We are told in Scripture that when the truth of God is our foundation, *peace* is our reward.

> *The Lord gives strength to his people; the Lord blesses*
> *His people with peace.*
> Psalm 29:11

However, peace can be tricky. Peace within a family, at school, at work, or between nations is not a guarantee in this life. How can our kids be content and have peace in such a troubled world? True peace can only be found in a relationship with Jesus Christ.

As our kids trek into adulthood, they will need to learn how to be content. Our kids will have to answer the questions, how will I be okay with *what is*? and, where will I find peace?

5. They will ask questions about *SUFFERING*. How will I cope with life?
   - *With alcohol?*
   - *With medications?*
   - *With relationships?*
   - *With God?*

So many kids today don't have any coping skills. This is evidenced in the high number of school shootings we have witnessed in the past ten years, and the many teen suicides. The violent state of our world today is tragic.

When trials come, and come they will, our kids need coping skills and they need to know where to go for comfort. We'll talk more about the importance of coping skills in Chapter 11,

> *He heals the brokenhearted and binds up their wounds.*
> Psalm 147:3

Teenagers need input from parents when deciding the answers to these critical life questions. They need a voice of truth regularly pointing them toward God.

By using the tools in this book, you can encourage your kids to answer the five life questions in a way that puts their life in God's hands.

- *Who am I?...I am a child of God (Galatians 3:26)*
- *Who will I live for?...I will live my life for God (Romans 12:1)*
- *What is truth?...God is truth (John 14:6)*
- *Where will I find peace?...I will find peace in God (Psalm 46:10)*
- *How will I cope with life?...God will get me through (Isaiah 41:10)*

Our role does change when our kids become teenagers. But we still have a role—a crucial role. And we still have influence.

> *"Parents are the frontline and most influential force in a teen's life."*
> –Mark Oestreicher

The noise of the world will never cease. And, the pull of the world is strong. Christian parents are young people's best chance of hearing truth and standing firm in their faith. Our kids may act as if we are irrelevant, but make no mistake, they are watching and they are listening.

So, just before your kids become teenagers, take a short breather and pat yourself on the back for a job well done. Then, prepare yourself for the hardest stage of parenting.

If you have teenagers, then you are almost done with the race. *Almost*. Don't give up so close to the finish line.

A Legacy of Complacency

Recently I was talking with a good friend of mine. I wanted to get her thoughts about passing on faith in Christ to our kids. Not only is she a great mom, but she is a single parent. I have great admiration for people who parent alone, yet still parent well. Parenting is hard enough without having to do it alone.

She comes from a long line of faithful people in her family. Her parents raised her to value her faith. But more importantly, to *live out* her faith. They raised her to treasure Scripture and to spend a lot of time on her knees. The legacy passed from generation to generation in her family was a legacy of a strong and active faith.

A couple years ago I was doing a Bible study by author, speaker, and Bible teacher, Beth Moore. The topic of the study had to do with breaking strongholds. One particular section was talking about family legacies and how to break free from them; family legacies that included things like abuse, rage, alcoholism, and unforgiveness.

Participants in the study were asked to think about how they would identify their family legacy.

Although my family history included some brokenness and dysfunction, it did not include abuse, or problems with drugs and alcohol, or anything quite so drastic. The legacy that my family passed down from generation to generation was a legacy of *complacency*. Basic faith may have been passed down through the generations, but not a radical surrender to a living God.

Although, not as openly destructive as some of these other strongholds, complacency is still a detestable thing.

So, because you are lukewarm—neither hot nor cold—
I am about to spit you out of my mouth.
Revelation 3:16

Satan has many tools in his toolbox. Obviously, he is pleased with the abuse, neglect, and dysfunction in so many families across the country. However, maybe even more dangerous are the tools that we don't see or recognize. The ones that lurk just under our radar. Ones like complacency.

According to Gotquestions.org, studies suggest a direct correlation between complacency in parents and duration of faith in their kids.

> One particular study found that when both parents were faithful and active in the church, ninety-three percent of their children remained faithful. When just one parent was faithful, seventy-three percent of their children remained faithful. When neither parent was particularly active in church, only fifty-three percent of their children stayed faithful. In those instances where neither parent was active at all and only attended church now and then, the percentage dropped to a mere six percent.[4]

I very much desired to pass on a radical, deep, surrendered faith in Christ to my kids, but felt woefully unequipped. I had the legacy of complacency in my lineage. I wasn't shown how to pass on a passionate faith in Christ to my children. Neither were my parents.

The posture of complacency is an epidemic in the American church today. Passionately faithful families are rare. Many of us have had to find this passion for ourselves before we could pass it on. We weren't taught from a young age the things that we now want to teach our kids. Therefore, we started with this mission late in the game.

Is it possible to change a family legacy? Is it possible to start a family legacy of radically and passionately seeking Christ? Anything is possible with Jesus Christ. It is *never* too late.

The Hearing

There are two aspects of passing on our faith that concern me the most. First, what are we speaking into our kids' lives. And second, what they are hearing and perceiving.

The following is a quote from Emma Smith, a student, from David Kinnaman's book, *You Lost Me. Why Young Christians are Leaving Church… and Rethinking Faith*.

> I want you to be someone I want to grow up to be like. I want you to step up and live by the Bible's standards. I want you to be inexplicably generous, unbelievably faithful, and radically committed. I want you to be a noticeably better person than my humanist teacher, than my atheist doctor, than my Hindu next-door neighbor. I want you to sell all you have and give it to the poor. I want you to not worry about your health like you're afraid of dying. I want you to live like you actually believe in the God you preach about. I don't want you to be like me; I want you to be like Jesus. That's when I'll start listening.[5]

These are powerful words straight from the mouth of a student. Doesn't this quote just say it all? How do such simple truths evade us? She is telling us the very way in which we get our youth to listen to us; and not just to get them listening, but *hearing*. We want them to hear our faith and breathe it in. We want them to believe us, and trust us enough to walk in our ways.

We must listen. We must respond. We must…

✓ *have integrity*
✓ *live by the Bible's standards*
✓ *be generous*
✓ *be faithful*
✓ *be radically committed*
✓ *be unconsumed with the worries of this world*

We must be like Jesus. Then, and only then, will our kids take our faith seriously.

The Bottom Line

Ultimately, it is God who reveals Himself to our children through the Holy Spirit. How and when that happens is not up to us. We can't force it. We can be a part of the process, but in the end, it is the work of each individual soul and the Holy Spirit.

Our kids belong to Him. They are God's children, just as we are. As much as we must surrender our lives to God, we must hand over our kids to Him also. We should do everything we can to teach our kids His ways, while putting all of our trust in Him, *not* in ourselves.

The scary truth is that we can do everything right, and produce a kid who doesn't choose to love or follow God. Or, we can do nothing at all to teach faith to our kids and produce a kid who becomes a powerful disciple of Christ.

However, as a Christian parent, I am going to do everything I can to tip the scales in favor of faith for my kids.

I waited thirty-five years to become a disciple of Christ. What a waste. Not thirty-five years to become a Christian. I have been a Christian all my life. It took that long to decide to become a disciple and *follow* Jesus.

Why did it take me so long to see how big and beyond measure God is? What had kept me blind all those years to a God who ached with love for me? How did I not see? How did I not know? Why did I not listen?

Looking back, I realize how disillusioned I was. Too many conflicting voices crowded the spaces of my mind. And moving forward, I want to make sure the loudest voices in my children's ears are God's and mine. I want them to hear truth.

Being involved in church is not enough to pass on our faith. Millennials and those following them in generation Z have no patience for the superficiality found in many American churches. If we continue to focus on the traditions and rituals of church, instead of living out our faith every day, our kids will likely walk away.

It is our job, as parents, to speak loudly to our children in the name of Jesus. If we don't, who will? If we leave it to our churches, our schools, or our communities, we will continue to lose our children to the world.

The world speaks loudly to our kids. It speaks through absent fathers, broken families, and childhood abuses. The world speaks loudly through public schools, movies, and social media. The world speaks loudly about the issues of pain, suffering, and morality. Our kids will listen to whoever is speaking the loudest to them, whether it is truth or not.

Our children will see a small God if that is what we show them. And, if we show them nothing at all about God, then they will blend into the world. They may come to know the Lord when they are older, or they may not.

My daughter will leave for college next year. Will she go off and be confident in her faith and join a church? Will she stay in love with Jesus? I don't know the answer to those questions. Time will tell. But I will do my best to reflect the person of Christ to my family.

Have I been the perfect model of Christ to my girls? Certainly not! Not even close. I have failed many times and in many ways as we all have.

Do I believe that God can make up for what I lack as a parent? Absolutely! As humans, *lack,* is our middle name. Thank goodness we have a God that is willing to take what little we have and add Himself to the equation to make something beautiful.

He has made everything beautiful in its time.
Ecclesiastes 3:11

Part I

The Elephant in the Room

Chapter 1

My Story: A Tale of Four Cousins

*"Every generation is pushing to be heard and understood, to find their own
way, to recover what they feel the previous generation fumbled away, and
to work out their parents' unfinished business."*[6]
—Hayden Shaw, *Generational IQ*

The world had changed. Families had changed. Values had changed.
The meaning of religion had changed. After I graduated from high
school twenty-six years ago, the world was not what I expected. The
moral landscape of college and life thereafter was hostile and foreign.

I struggled when the faith of my childhood didn't translate smoothly into
adulthood. I was disillusioned when the formulas of faith and church that I
had always known no longer worked. The messiness of life, the difficulty
of marriage and relationships, and the many ups and downs I experienced
overwhelmed me. My faith couldn't handle it. And I walked away.

The Four of Us

My childhood was spent with my brother and two cousins. The four of us grew up together. Every Thanksgiving and Christmas we came down to Indiana to see them from where we lived in Michigan. We went on summer vacations together and to each other's church camps. As kids, we created haunted houses and puppet shows, and played football in the fields outside of my Granddad's house. Many warm summer evenings were spent chasing fireflies out in the cornfields, together, the four of us.

My brother, Greg, and I grew up in Farmington Hills, Michigan, a suburb of Detroit. Church was a significant part of our life. We went faithfully on Sundays, Wednesday nights, and holidays. And my brother and I never missed a youth group activity, Christian concert, retreat, or mission trip. We were fully immersed in the Evangelical life.

At the age of sixteen, Greg felt called by God to the mission field. After graduation, He went on to attend a Christian college in Chicago and followed that with seventeen years in the mission field in southern Mexico.

When I left home and went to college three years later, however, my faith did not follow me there. The faith of my childhood and the real world I later encountered, didn't seem to fit together. So I did what most youth group graduates did, and left my faith behind.

My cousins were leaders in their youth group in high school and both went to Christian colleges. My aunt and uncle were very involved in the church. Church life was their whole life. And their youth group was like their extended family.

They had a strong passion for God. Many evenings during holiday visits or at Lake Tippecanoe, where we vacationed together in the summer, were spent engrossed in deep, philosophical discussions about all things spiritual.

As I look back, religion was a big part of who we were. Church was central to our lives.

Fast forward thirty years and only *one* out of the four of us never left the faith or the church. *One out of four!* I walked away and have since come back to the Lord. But neither of my two cousins, who were so spiritual in their youth, raised their kids in the church.

Many young evangelical generation Xers and millennials share my story.

Now, I have two daughters growing up in the same environment as I did. Many nights I lie awake thinking, "What will my girls do when they leave our home? Have I done enough to pass on my faith?"

As my kids approach high school graduation, it is sad for me to think about them leaving home. However, it is far more terrifying to think that they could leave home and turn their backs on God and the church.

A Hot Mess

I was somewhat of a hot mess sixteen years ago when I had my first child. I was also very unaware of the issues from my past that were bubbling up just under the surface. I was like an unsuspecting bystander in my own life. And I was blindsided; hit by the bus of emotional scars from childhood. I am living proof that unresolved issues or baggage in our lives don't just go away, they accumulate. And when we are most vulnerable, they come out to bite us in the butt!

My parents divorced when I was eight, and poof, just like that, my family no longer existed. New families emerged, but mine was gone.

During the 70s, divorce was on the rise at an alarming rate. The number of divorces almost doubled until 1980, when divorce rates finally began to fall.[7] It was "The Great Experiment" of the baby boomer generation. And I, along with many other kids, was the guinea pig.

No one knew the long term consequences divorce would have on kids.

Now, twenty and thirty years down the road, we know that divorce is devastating to children and the adults they become. Ripple effects can be seen far and wide.

Issues of abandonment, low self-worth, and lack of identity haunted me. I left my childhood home with no real foundation. And I went out into the world very much lost.

The more self-discovery I did, through contemplation and the Holy Spirit, the more I realized I had holes in me. The broken home that I came from left me with a deficit. It's an unintentional, yet almost unavoidable, consequence of divorce.

Holes left from childhood make life very difficult as an adult.

I didn't want my kids growing up with these holes. I didn't want my kids to live with regret, feel like a disappointment, or feel less than the amazing children of God that they were. I wanted them to be *whole*.

Around year fourteen in our marriage, my husband and I went through a period of intense crisis. There were many times I wasn't sure if we were going to make it. We both had a lot of baggage from our childhood.

As I look back on it, I see myself flapping and flailing while treading the stormy waters of pain and suffering. Being tossed about and nearly being sucked under.

Huge waves of shame, rejection, and loneliness threatened to overtake me. Water drenched my face from all directions. The sting of disappointment, loss, and depression filled my lungs as I gasped for breath. Salt entered all the wounds of my bloodied body and pain overcame me. Sharks were circling.

And in the midst of the chaos, I cried out to God. Very much like David did.

In my distress I called to the Lord; I cried to my God for help. From His temple He heard my voice; my cry came before Him, into His ears.
Psalm 18:6

Through the storm, I never let go of God's hand, and He never let go of mine. God was so faithful and true to His promises.

The Lord your God goes with you; He will never leave you nor forsake you.
Deuteronomy 31:6

My husband and I trusted God when it seemed like all was lost. We trusted Him against all odds. We trusted Him when our strength was nearly gone. And when it seemed like everyone else was choosing the easy way, we walked into the eye of the storm.

I am not saying it was easy, because it wasn't. I am not saying it wasn't messy, and we never wanted to give up, because it was and we did. The storm seemed to last forever.

But I can say that we came out on the other side better, stronger, and more trusting in God than ever before. We had been through the Refiner's fire, and we were better for it.

Having overcome such a huge storm, we started to see what a *BIG* God we served. Pain has a way of opening our eyes to more of the divine.

Pain has a way of opening our eyes to more of the divine.

Since then, God has ignited a fire within me that I cannot quench. He has been filling me with His grace, goodness, and the power of His Word. I have been absolutely raw to receiving more of Him with eagerness and anticipation. Sometimes all I can see is Him. He is beautiful, and He is enough.

> *Now to Him who is able to do immeasurably more than all we ask or*
> *imagine, according to His power that is at work within us.*
> Ephesians 3:20

Pouring In

I had some definite and undeniable holes in me from my childhood. I felt like swiss cheese, pocked with the marks of missing pieces. I knew something was missing. I just didn't know what or why.

My awareness of my "hole-y-ness" *(not holiness)*, or being "full of holes," led me to explore the concept of *pouring in* to another person as God has poured Himself into us.

> *And He has filled him with the Spirit of God, in wisdom, in*
> *understanding and in knowledge and in all craftsmanship.*
> Exodus 35:31 (NASB)

As disciples of Christ, we should always be pouring into each other; pouring in our love, and pouring in Christ. We do not get to just hold Jesus for ourselves. The spirit of God needs to be moving in and out of His people.

And, we must pour our very "self" into our kids.

The image of pouring into my kids has always been at the forefront of my mind. Anytime I say "you are beautiful" or "you are my sunshine" or "I delight in you," to my girls, I am *pouring in* to them. I can see it in their eyes. Their love tank is filling up.

A couple summers ago I did a Beth Moore Bible study on 1 and 2 Thessalonians called *Children of the Day*. One particular video segment stuck with me. Moore posed a question. "Are you missing peace in your life? A missing *piece* is a missing *peace*." Then she illustrated what she called, "no holes parenting."

According to Moore, to be a healthy child of God everyone needs six things from their parents.

1. To be nurtured
2. To be affectionately desired
3. Accepting parents' very self (to be poured into)
4. To be exhorted
5. To be encouraged
6. To be charged to walk in a manner worthy of God[8]

This is what it means to *pour in* to our children. We must pour in these six things.

We nurture them with love and care. And we affectionately desire our kids. We delight in them, rather than just tolerating them. However, not all children experience this from a parent. But we are *all* affectionately desired by God. He can give to a child what they lack from a parent.

Paul talks about pouring in when writing to the Thessalonians. He shared his very "self."

So, being affectionately desirous of you, we were ready to share with you not only the gospel of God but also our own selves, because you had become very dear to us.
1 Thessalonians 2:8 (ESV)

We pour our "own selves" into our children. We exhort, encourage, and charge them to walk in a manner worthy of God. As parents, we pour our life into them; our experiences and wisdom, our time and treasure, our love and acceptance, our message and purpose, and our very souls. We pour in our love of Christ. Everything we have and everything we are, we pour into our children.

Looking at the list, I know which ones that I need to work on. I am so thankful we don't have to be a perfect parent, because we never can be. Our kids already have a perfect parent in God.

Three Things Every Human Soul Needs

Pouring in is probing. Pouring in is listening. Pouring in is seeking to know our kids at a soul level. It is searching for the child of God that is in each one of our kids.

Now that we understand how important it is to *pour in* to our kids, we need a plan. How do we feed the souls of our kids every day?

In addition to being loved, three of the greatest longings of the human soul are to be *seen, heard,* and *known.* It is no different for our kids, whether they are five, fifteen, or twenty-five.

1. The human soul longs to be *SEEN.* God sees us.

Whether it is in the joys and the celebrations of the soul, or in the difficult times of life, we all long to be seen. This desire makes us human and unites us all.

I recently watched the movie, *Hidden Figures,* about African American women mathematicians who worked at NASA in 1961. They were "computers" before there were computers. Three women in particular were pivotal to the space program, Katherine Johnson, Mary Jackson, and Dorothy Vaughan.

At the time, however, segregation was still very much a part of American society. What must it have felt like to be these brilliant woman and not be seen? Or, not be recognized for their contributions?

Every human being longs to be seen. God made us with this longing because He sees us.

In the movie, *Avatar,* the Na'vi people who inhabit the far away world of Pandora, say "I see you" instead of "I love you." This shows the power of being seen. Here, being seen is equated with love.

There are many names of God, however, the most beautiful to me is El Roi, The God who Sees.

This name is first used in the story in Genesis 16 where Sarai couldn't conceive a child and in desperation, offers Hagar, her slave, to her husband, Abram. What ensues is a mess, which is usually what happens when we take matters into our own hands instead of waiting on God.

Sarai mistreats Hagar, so she flees. And God finds her beside a desert spring.

After a conversation with God, Hagar calls Him, *El Roi,* which is Hebrew for, "the God Who sees." She was the only person in Scripture to give God a name.

She gave this name to the Lord who spoke to her: "You are the God who
sees me," for she said, "I have now seen the One who sees me."
Genesis 16:13

He is **El Roi**, the God Who sees

He sees me, and He sees you.

For the eyes of the Lord range throughout the earth to strengthen those
whose hearts are fully committed to him.
2 Chronicles 16:9

We need to make an effort to really see our teenagers and young people in the church and the community. They are beautiful souls made in the image of God. And they are an important part of our churches.

Kara Powell, Jake Mulder, and Brad Griffin, put it this way in their book, *Growing Young*, "Young people…don't want to sit passively on the sidelines but are drawn to churches and leaders who help them get in the game."[9]

2. The human soul longs to be *HEARD*. God hears us.

The eyes of the Lord are on the righteous, and His ears are
attentive to their prayer.
1 Peter 3:12

I was with a friend recently who had just been to a family reunion. She teared up when she told me that she often spends days with her family without anyone asking her what is going on in her life. She said, "never being heard crushes your soul."

According to writer and speaker Steven Argue, who has a PhD from Michigan State University and is the Applied Research Strategist for the Fuller Youth Institute, the three most important words to use with our children and youth in general are, "tell me more."

I think we need to remember as parents that the first question isn't as important as the second or third question. A first question usually comes from our own agenda—we want information, clarity, or context. Second and third questions are responsive questions that emerge from the conversation. They show our kids how well we're listening and really seeking to understand, rather than just interrogate…Maybe for us, "tell me more" is more of a posture than a solo question![10]

We must hear our kids. This means not just listening, but *hearing* and sometimes probing. We must turn off our devices or the TV when our kids are talking to us. They deserve our time and undivided attention. This is how we feed their soul.

And young people must be heard in our churches as well.

3.   The human soul longs to be *KNOWN*. God knows us.

The human soul longs to be known—known to our bones. We want someone to see the good, the bad, and the ugly inside us, and still love us. We don't have to hide with God, because he knows us intimately.

> *Before I formed you in the womb I knew you*
> Jeremiah 1:5

> *"Being truly known, loved, and accepted is what we all long for."*[11]
> –David Kinnaman and Gabe Lyons, *Good Faith*

Do we take the time to really *know* our kids? Do we seek to know our teenagers? Do we desire to know the young people at our churches? Or, do we dismiss them because they are young?

Pouring into our kids requires that we *see* them. It requires that we *hear* them. And it requires that we seek to really *know* them. These are the things that will feed their soul, and cause them to be open to the gospel.

Chapter 2

Houston, We Have a Problem

"Should we worry about the end of Christianity as we know it? Is the church heading toward a massive decline? Will we lose an entire generation?...Here's the bottom line: It is not as bad as we've heard, but it was never as good as we thought. And it's declining, especially with the Millennials."[12]
—Hayden Shaw, *Generational IQ*

The human race is a curious one.

I remember growing up watching the TV series, *Cosmos*, with Carl Sagan with my family. The show was the most watched series on American public television in the 1980s. It had an audience of four hundred million people in sixty countries all over the world.[13]

What would it be like to be in space? How would the realization of being so far from home strike NASA's brave men and women as earth floats by outside the space shuttles' windows? *With excitement? With awe? With*

13

terror? It would certainly take your breath away. How stunning the beautiful, blue, jewel floating in the darkness would seem.

I can't even begin to imagine what the astronauts on April 13th, 1970, two days into the Apollo 13 mission must have felt when the unthinkable happened and the master alarm started flashing. Insulation around a wire inside the liquid oxygen tank had been lost, igniting an explosion. It blew out the side of the service module causing power loss and an oxygen leak.[14]

The movie, *Apollo 13*, depicted so well James Lovell's famous quote to mission control, *"Houston, we have a problem."* Which they changed from the actual quote, *"Houston, we've had a problem."*[15] Talk about a monumental movie quote. And, a monumental understatement for that matter! Lovell, along with Jack Swigert and Fred Haise, knew the severity of the situation. It was life or death. If they couldn't fix the problem, the next moments would be their last.

For most of us back on earth, our lives and jobs are far less intense. We have to go to the movies to get that kind of excitement. Most of our lives don't involve much risk. And sometimes, we find ourselves coasting mindlessly through life on autopilot. We need to wake up.

Author and speaker Josh McDowell wrote in his book, *The Last Christian Generation:*

> I sincerely believe unless something is done now to change the spiritual state of our young people—*you* will become the last Christian generation![16]

That was written in 2006, over ten years ago.

Has the landscape of Christian youth drastically changed since then? Certainly not. The problem persists. And with an ever-growing intolerance for Christianity in our schools, universities, and government, not to mention the threat to religious freedom for small businesses, we must protect and preserve the faith of our kids.

"Seventy-five percent of young adults raised in a Christian home leave the church after they leave the home. Think about that—on average, three out of every four kids attending your youth group won't be attending any church a few years from now." [17]
—Frank Turek

Can you see the master alarm flashing?

We Are Losing Our Kids

Every time I have the opportunity to talk with other parents in the church about this topic, I can see the fear in their eyes. *Timely* is the word used most often in those conversations. The topic of kids leaving the church resonates with most Christian parents today.

"There is a deep, abiding fear among Christian parents that their kids, having been raised in a Christian family and having spent their childhood and teenage years in the church, will nonetheless walk away from God." [18]
—Josh McDowell and Sean McDowell, *The Unshakable Truth*

That deep, abiding fear is what prompted the writing of this book. Have my kids accepted Christ as their Savior? Yes. Have my kids been baptized? Yes. Is their faith strong enough to withstand opposition in college and the real world? I don't know.

My girls are good kids. They love God, love our church and love our family.

However, as I looked around at the youth in my church, something seemed very wrong, yet very familiar. The young people didn't seem to be prioritizing their faith. And it occurred to me what I was actually witnessing. They were just like us.

Our churches may look good and appear to be growing. They may have fellowship, and good teaching. And, our churches may have exciting and dynamic youth group programs. But do these components contribute to a healthy thriving faith in our young people?

Good churches and good Christian families aren't necessarily, affectively passing on faith to their young people.

I found this quote by author, speaker, and founder of Prison Fellowship, Chuck Colson in a promotional video for a local ministry called Anchorsaway (www.anchorsaway.org) that equips teenagers with the truth of the gospel and educates them about apologetics and worldviews.

Teaching kids to defend their faith when they get away from the home and church and into college, let me tell you, that is a mission field. That ought to be our number one mission field because we are discovering that the vast majority of kids coming out of youth groups and churches, good churches, and good families, they're lost when they get to campus and so many of them lose their faith.

According to Brett Kunkle, the Student Impact Director at Stand to Reason (www.str.org), "Barna has the number at sixty-one percent. Lifeway has it at seventy percent. Even if we take Barna's lower number and then subtract another ten percent just to be conservative, we're still left with a situation where we are losing half our kids."[19]

Barna Group is a leading research organization focused on the intersection of faith and culture. And LifeWay Research conducts frequent surveys on today's church and culture.

Though the numbers may vary slightly from one study to the next, they all come to the same conclusion—*we are losing our kids*. It is undeniable that a majority of kids raised in Christian homes leave the faith when they leave their homes.

Already Gone

Last summer I had a conversation with a friend at church who was concerned because her son, a junior in high school, was becoming disengaged from the church youth group. He would sit in the donut area outside the youth room instead of participating with the other students.

While he might have been the only one sitting there, many churched kids are disengaged from the faith, some who come to youth group, and some who stay home. But many are, as Ken Ham and Britt Beemer called their book, *Already Gone.*

> Based on interviews with twenty-two thousand adults and over two thousand teenagers in twenty-five separate surveys, George Barna unquestionably quantified the seriousness of the situation: six out of ten twenty-somethings who were involved in a church during their teen years are already gone.[20]

Many times I have reminisced on my experience growing up in the Evangelical church. And as I look around at the young people in my church today, they aren't much different than I was thirty years ago, right before I walked away.

What we were doing didn't work then, and it doesn't work now. Church is not sticking to most young people.

> *"A majority of twenty-somethings—sixty-one percent of today's young adults—had been churched at one point during their teen years but they are now spiritually disengaged (i.e., not actively attending church, reading the Bible or praying)."[21]*
> –George Barna

Would you be surprised to know that of the kids that left the church, only eleven percent did so in college? Did you know that almost ninety percent were lost in middle and high school? And about forty percent are leaving the church in *elementary* and *middle school.*[22] Often, by the time we are alarmed about the situation, our kids are already gone.

According to Dr. Kara Powell and Dr. Chap Clark in their book, *Sticky Faith,* "Your kids' faith trajectories are formed long before twelfth grade."[23]

Are They Returning?

Do the kids that leave the church after leaving home ever return? The answer is *yes,* some do return to church as they get into their late twenties, marry, and start a family.

However, according to Dr. Kara Powell and Dr. Chap Clark, in their book, *Sticky Faith,* based on research from The Fuller Youth Institute between forty and seventy percent of youth group graduates who abandon their faith and the church, won't return.[24]

Christian Doctrine Matters

Not only are our kids leaving the faith, but studies also show that our kids are not understanding the doctrine of Christianity. Or, it's not taught in an effective way such that they believe it to be true.

*"Our research shows that most young people lack a deep
understanding of their faith."*[25]
—David Kinnaman, *You Lost Me*

- Eighty-five percent of youth from Christian homes who attend public schools do not embrace a Christian worldview[26]
- Fifty-eight percent believe all faiths teach equally valid truths
- Sixty-three percent don't believe Jesus is the Son of the one true God
- Fifty-one percent don't believe Jesus rose from the dead
- Sixty-five percent don't believe Satan is real
- Sixty-eight percent don't believe the Holy Spirit is real[27]

These statistics are staggering. How could we as Christian parents and the church be producing kids that have gotten it so wrong?

Is the Church Reaching Young People?

Kara Powell, Jake Mulder, and Brad Griffin state in their book, *Growing Young*: "Young people need a thriving church. A thriving church both grounds them in community and sends them out to serve."[28]

Sadly, according to their research, "no major Christian tradition is growing in the US today."[29] Young people have been dropping out of church for decades.

We hope that our kids make friends and feel like they fit in at youth group. We all know that some kids go to church to hang out with their friends. Some go because they like the games and music. And some kids go because they value church and love the Lord.

Whatever the reason, we are happy if they are just going. However, should we be concerned if our kids are spiritually disengaged even if they do go to church?

The College Experience

What is the "college experience?" Though both my husband and I have our bachelor's degrees and went to the same university, we had very different experiences of college.

For the most part, I enjoyed college. I went alone and didn't know anybody. I saw college as a fresh start. I lived in the dorms and apartments, had multiple roommates, stayed on campus for most weekends, participated in clubs, went to parties, and was exposed to many different kinds of people and many different philosophies of life. Freedom was the greatest part of college for me.

My home life that I left behind was somewhat tumultuous. My parents divorced when I was eight and both remarried. I didn't feel like I quite fit into my dad's new family. And my step dad and I were constantly fighting.

Although my husband's parents were also divorced and remarried, he didn't feel the need to escape. So, he went to college while living at home and working. His experience was more like an extension of high school.

We have many household discussions about the value, *or lack thereof,* of "the college experience." I want our girls to experience roommates, dorm activities, cafeteria food, and walking a beautiful campus. To me, foraging for food on Sunday nights when the cafeteria was closed, and hitting my parents up for quarters to do laundry was part of being a college student. Jamie never had any of that. He is more concerned about the binge drinking and partying that is so prevalent on college campuses.

The truth is, both of us are right. College can be a positive experience where you meet lifelong friends and establish independence. It is a time of trying new things, and having fun while you're young. And college is a good stepping stone toward independence.

However, research shows that kids are vulnerable at college. Vulnerable to destructive behavior and vulnerable to losing their faith. Is the college experience beneficial for kids? Or, has it become too dangerous?

According to Dr. Kara Powell and Dr. Chap Clark, in their book, *Sticky Faith* there is cause for concern. "Each month, just under fifty percent of full-time college students binge drink, abuse prescription drugs, and/or abuse illegal drugs."[30] They also found that one hundred percent of the sixty-nine youth group graduates they surveyed drank alcohol during their first few years of college.[31]

If you asked me, one hundred percent of any group over ten, doing anything, is remarkable. Not one kid in the survey abstained from alcohol their first years away from home. *Not one!*

The medical communities in college towns are painfully aware of the habits of college students. Dr. Michael Kimmel, professor of sociology at State University of New York, researched extensively the behaviors of college students and the likely outcomes of their destructive behavior.

Every single emergency room in every single hospital adjoining or near a college campus stocks extra supplies on Thursday nights—rape kits for the sexual assault victims, IV fluids for those who are dehydrated from alcohol-induced vomiting, and blood for drunk driving accidents.[32]

And there is also the fear of our kids losing their faith in college.

Author and filmmaker, Dinesh D'Souza in his book, *What's So Great About Christianity?* comments on the college environment and faith.

Parents invest a good portion of their life savings in college education and entrust their offspring to people who are supposed to educate them. Isn't it wonderful that educators have figured out a way to make parents the instruments of their own undoing? Isn't it brilliant that they have persuaded Christian moms and dads to finance the destruction of their own beliefs and values? Who said atheists aren't clever?

In 2007, two Jewish researchers conducted a survey regarding attitudes of college professors. They found that "the most disliked students by college professors are evangelical Christians. More than half (fifty-three percent) of all college professors view evangelical students unfavorably."[33]
When we send our kids to college, are we throwing them to the wolves?

Reality Check

One of my mantras in life is, *it is what it is*. In other words, panicking is rarely, if ever, helpful. And being paralyzed with fear keeps us stuck.

We serve a God who is bigger than any statistic and above any reality we face in this world. Sometimes we have to be reminded of how big our God is.

Imagine God with a body. Imagine our entire universe being squeezed into a bubble, and inserted into one cell of His "body." Did you know there are roughly 37.2 *trillion* cells in the human body! *And that doesn't include bacteria!*[34]

God is tremendous, colossal, massive and immense. His abilities and reach are unmatched by anyone or anything. And it's with good reason that God tells us in Scripture not to worry.

Do not be anxious about anything, but in every situation, by prayer and petition, with thanksgiving, present your requests to God. And the peace of God, which transcends all understanding, will guard your hearts and your minds in Christ Jesus.
Philippians 4:6-7

The Lord knew this would be the state of things from the moment He created birds of the air and fish of the sea. He knew everything we would ever do before any human being ever walked the earth. In other words, *God's got this!*

In this world you will have trouble. But take heart! I have overcome the world.
John 16:33

However, we must do our part and teach God's Word to our kids. We are their best chance of knowing Jesus and adopting the faith.

You have known the Holy Scriptures, which are able to make you wise for salvation through faith in Christ Jesus.
2 Timothy 3:15

My family and I live in Indianapolis and we love our Sunday afternoon football. There is nothing more relaxing than an afternoon on the couch with a Colts game on. It is a tradition in our family and we fiercely protect it. *Don't mess with my Sundays!*

Our Colts weren't so hot this season. One of the games was played entirely on our side of the field. When they displayed the stats during the second half, it was embarrassing how little we had the ball. Not only is the defensive line exhausted when this happens, but we never get anywhere. If we can't get our quarterback, Andrew Luck, out on the field, we aren't going to score any points.

Often in life we find ourselves stuck on the defensive. Simply reacting and protecting. Settling for the status quo. We figure, if we raise our kids and they haven't smoked pot, gotten drunk, had sex, or broken the law, then we're good.

We need to raise the bar.

When it comes to passing on our faith to the next generation, we must be *proactive* not merely *reactive*. We must get that quarterback on the field and push *forward* if we want to win.

Chapter 3

Why are Our Kids Leaving the Church?
Digging in the Soil

"The Christian community needs a new mind—a new way of thinking, a new way of relating, a new vision of our role in the world—to pass on the faith to this and future generations."[35]
—David Kinnaman, *You Lost Me*

Why are our kids leaving the church? There lies the million dollar question! It's a simple question with a far from simple answer. Just like there were many factors that played into our faith journeys, there are many factors that play into the faith journeys of our kids. It is often complicated and messy. And ultimately, only God knows what twists and turns our kids will make on their way to the cross.

As we learned in the last chapter, most kids don't leave home with a personal, powerful, and passionate faith in Jesus Christ. Faith that is not claimed personally will most often be lost.

I grew up heavily involved in church, yet my mind wasn't really renewed.

> *Do not conform to the pattern of this world,*
> *but be transformed by the renewing of your mind.*
> Romans 12:2

My eyes weren't opened to Him so that I could see.

> *Open my eyes that I may see wonderful things in your law.*
> Psalm 119:18

And, I did not seek to partake of the divine nature.

> *He has given us His very great and precious promises, so that through them*
> *you may participate in the divine nature.*
> 2 Peter 1:4

I have been a Christian most of my life, but I haven't always followed Jesus. Why did I not see who was before me? This question has plagued me for decades.

The Greatest Show on Earth

Young people in the 80s and 90s were pumped up on the drug of faith. We had our high. And as with any high, we eventually came crashing down. We were in a kind of "honeymoon phase" of our faith. And nobody told us that the honeymoon would end.

Matt Bays expressed similar disillusionment with his faith growing up in the church in his book, *Finding God in the Ruins*.

In time it would seem as though we'd all been given free tickets to The Greatest Show on Earth, and then when we arrived, nothing. No popcorn or lions. No ringmaster with a long whip strapped to his side. No trapeze, no high dive, no clowns, and no one being shot out of a cannon. Before we were saved, the preshow was exciting. But once we entered the Big Top, we found less pomp and more circumstance. We'd been had.[36]

Somehow, the message of faith got lost in translation for many gen X'ers like Matt and myself. The trend continues with millennials and now, with what some are calling, generation Z.

When "churched" kids go out on their own and decide for themselves how they will spend their lives, following Christ often doesn't make the cut. *Why?*

There are many theories on what causes kids to leave the church. However, I believe Josh McDowell said it best in his book, *The Last Christian Generation*.

The obvious but, nonetheless, shocking truth is that we are not seeing the majority of our churched youth transformed by the power of God…the majority of our young people appear neither to understand who the true God is nor the true meaning of Christianity.[37]

Kids who grow up in the church leave the faith primarily for three reasons. First, they are not being transformed by the power of God. An inner transformation must happen when the Holy Spirit enters us. We are changed. We are made new. And most of our kids fail to go through this transformation.

Second, they do not understand who the true God is. Research has shown that kids growing up in the church are not understanding who the God of the Bible is. To follow Christ means to seek to *know* Him and pursue Him with everything we have. Once we are introduced to the person of Christ, we spend the rest of our lives seeking to know Him more.

And third, they do not understand what it means to be a Christian. Our lives as followers of Christ should reflect *Him*. We need to look like followers of Christ in our everyday lives. Our kids may be Christians, but a majority of them are not living out a Biblical worldview (more about worldviews in Chapter 14).

Digging Deeper

It has been the most unusual February in the Midwest. We have had a record number of days over sixty degrees. And, I have spent a lot of time on our patio, enjoying the spring-like weather.

As I sit in the warm sun, I look around at the yard and fantasize as I often do about the paradise it *could* be. Our yard has a lot of potential. Several years before we moved in, the previous owners put in a beautiful patio and had professional landscaping done. We lucked out. It meant that we didn't have to do it.

However, that was eleven years ago and a lot of living has happened here since then. I would be embarrassed if the previous owners saw the yard now. Life has taken many unforeseen, and expensive, twists and turns. The yard was never a priority.

My mind wanders to, *where should we put the garden? The area around the fire pit needs to be cleaned up. The raspberry patch is overgrown, it needs to be pruned.* And I dream about the trees that we planted five years ago being twenty feet tall, full and beautiful.

When we first moved to our current home, we planted several different kinds of maple trees. Autumn is our favorite season and we longed to have a beautiful array of color outside our windows to enjoy.

The elementary school my kids went to gave every student a maple tree in the fourth grade. When Emily brought hers home, it was just a stick about two feet tall. At the time, we were still trying to grow our yard with trees, so we thought, *why not?* So we planted it.

It grew by leaps and bounds every year. Much faster than the ones we had bought and planted years ago. In the years that followed, small maple trees started popping up in our landscaping. Five or six a year would volunteer from Emily's tree in our yard. And they grew and thrived. So we replanted many of them.

Today, these trees that volunteered are much bigger than the ones we planted ten years ago. *Why?* What made these thrive when the others didn't?

It takes just the right formula in the ground for trees to grow. The amount of sun or shade and the amount of moisture make a difference. Also the ph, acidity, certain trace elements like boron, copper, iron, chloride, manganese, molybdenum, and zinc must be present in just the right amounts.

What was the exact formula for this type of maple tree? I couldn't begin to tell you. But, whatever it was, our yard had it! Trees grew and grew. The original tree that we planted from Emily's fourth grade class is now taller than the house. It is beautiful and produces shade for our patio.

If we really want to get to the bottom of the problem of the spirituality of our kids then we must dig deep and look at the soil. Are we applying the right elements?

Some of our kids are like trees that do not grow and thrive. Something is wrong with the soil in which the gospel is planted. Something is keeping their spirituality from developing and transforming them.

Let's look at a parable in Scripture that we all know well; the parable of the sower.

A farmer went out to sow his seed. As he was scattering the seed, some fell along the path; it was trampled on, and the birds ate it up. Some fell on rocky ground, and when it came up, the plants withered because they had no moisture. Other seed fell among thorns, which grew up with it and choked the plants. Still other seed fell on good soil. It came up and yielded a crop, a hundred times more than was sown.

Luke 8:5-8

This parable explains the problem we face with our kids. It describes four scenarios for those who hear the gospel and four ways to respond to it.

1. We can hear it, and reject it

2. We can hear it, and are tested and fail
3. We can hear it, but never mature, or
4. We can hear it, and become fruitful

Kids who have grown up in the church are *hearers* of the gospel. Their parents have taken them to church, Sunday school, youth group, vacation bible school, and church camps. Church has always been a considerable part of their childhood.

The seed is the gospel of Jesus Christ that we receive that causes us to grow. Without the seed, nothing will grow in our soil. The seed requires water, nutrients, and sunlight in order to grow into a plant. We must nurture the soil of our kids' faith, so it can grow and be fruitful.

Let's look at four kids that illustrate this parable.

Scenario #1: Our kids can hear it and reject it.

A farmer went out to sow his seed. As he was scattering the seed, some fell along the path; it was trampled on, and the birds ate it up. (v.5)

Samantha has grown up in a family that doesn't practice any religion. Her parents have never taken her and her sisters to church. They are "Chreasters" (those who only go to church on Christmas and Easter). After her grandpa dies during her junior year, her mom starts going to church with a friend from work and she becomes a Christian and gets baptized. Her mom is excited about her new-found faith and talks about it all the time. She tries talking to her husband and Samantha about it, but they are not interested. *Why is mom all weird about this new "religion" thing?* Samantha wonders.

Samantha's mom tries to talk to her about Jesus, but she flat out rejects it. Seeds are scattered, but they fall on the path. Samantha believes that there are many ways to get to God, and many names to call him. *Why do we need to pick one over the other?* she argues. *A religion that works for one person might not work for another,* she says. Believing in Jesus might be good for Samantha's mom, but it's not for her.

The seeds are trampled and eaten by birds. A plant never grows.

Scenario #2: Our kids can hear it and are tested and fail.

Some fell on rocky ground, and when it came up, the plants withered because they had no moisture. (v.6)

Sean's family is catholic. His parents have always taken him to mass at St. Luke's. They are good people with good values, and they figure that is good enough. Spirituality doesn't affect their daily lives very much.

Sean meets a new kid at school. He is really cool and they start hanging out together and become friends. He seems like a nice enough kid. Sean starts skipping youth group to hang out with him.

His new friend is into Hinduism and talks about it often. He teaches Sean about reincarnation, the cycles of creation, and Karma. *A thornbush next to the little plant begins to grow.* As Sean learns more about Hinduism his interest is peaked. He does more research on Hinduism and researches Buddhism as well. He learns about various gods and things like, Brahma, enlightenment, and zen. He reads that there are many names for God and many ways to get to the afterlife. He had never heard that before.

Sean and his new friend start to hang out with more kids that practice Eastern religions. One day, Sean announces to his parents that he is a Buddhist and he no longer wants to go to church. *The thorn bushes soak up all the rich nutrients in the soil leaving none for the little plant of faith.* His parents argue with him on Sunday mornings. They beg him to go to church. They even make a desperate plea for help from their priest, but eventually they give up. Sean's parents nervously hope that he'll come back to the faith someday when he starts a family. *The little plant is choked out by the thorn bushes.*

When nutrients disappear the plant dries up because it has not yet become strong enough. Its roots are not very deep.

Scenario #3: Our kids can hear it, but never mature.

*Other seed fell among thorns, which grew up with it
and choked the plants. (v.7)*

Seeds are once again thrown out onto the soil. And once again a kid receives it and a plant starts to grow.

It is Michael's senior year. This is the year to celebrate the accomplishment of twelve years of school and acceptance into college. This is what he has worked so hard for. He is ready to move out and be independent. He is eagerly anticipating this new season of life.

Michael had grown up in the church and always attended youth group. He has been a leader the last two years and went on most of the mission trips. His best friends are church friends and they are like brothers. He loves the worship music and the games.

He and his family are always at church. Even though faith isn't discussed much at home, they all know that church is important.

Summer passes quickly and the time to go to college is finally here. He moves into his dorm and meets his new roommate. *He seems okay*, he thinks to himself. Classes start and the semester is off and running. He is officially a college student!

The frat house on Pearl Street is having a party on Saturday. Some guys from his floor are going, and ask Michael if he wants to come. *A thornbush next to the little plant begins to grow*. The house is packed and the beat of loud music vibrates in his chest. Someone hands Michael a beer, before he can say no. He shrugs his shoulders and thinks, *one drink won't hurt anything.*

Through his freshman year, Michael dates a girl he meets in one of his classes. She is amazing and he is head over heels in love. Things are getting pretty serious and one night, it happens. In the heat of the moment, they go too far. Michael has always said that he is going to wait until marriage. *What happened?*

Years pass, and Michael dates many girls. He fails over and over again to maintain his purity. He finally gives up. *I just can't do it*, he thinks to himself. *The little plant is choked out by the thorn-bushes.* The Thursday night Christian group he had started out going to is replaced by going to the bar with his buddies.

His dad used to tell him that it was wise to be home by ten o'clock every night, even in college. "We do most of the things we regret in college after ten p.m., it is easier to sin in the dark," he would say. Michael is finding out how true that is.

By the time Michael graduates, he has become quite a drinker. He has lost his conviction for purity before marriage and no longer goes to church. He is swept up by the allure of the world. And he leaves his faith in the dust.

Scenario #4: Our kids can hear it, and become fruitful.

> *Still other seed fell on good soil. It came up and yielded a crop,*
> *a hundred times more than was sown. (v.8)*

A parent has been spending much time tilling and fertilizing the ground. The soil is rich in the right nutrients and minerals. After being watered frequently, the soil is very moist. Once the seed is tossed to the ground, the plant begins to grow in the fertile soil. Its roots easily reach far down into the earth, gleaning from the rich source of water below. It grows quickly into a lush, healthy plant and produces fruit.

Prayer and Scripture are an important part of Rachel's family life. They often do devotions at dinner where they read and discuss Scripture. Her parents quote Scripture and talk about how it relates to various situations that come up at work or school. This helps Rachel connect her faith with her life.

Rachel always knew her mom got up at 5:30 every morning to read the Bible. Her mom had done this as long as she could remember. Her parents were very compassionate to the poor and to those in need. Her mom adopted an inmate at a prison nearby and treated him like her own son. She talked on the phone with him and sent him care packages. Several nights a week, they would have people over for dinner or to spend the night.

She often sees her parents praying together when things are tough. Rachel knows that her parents love God. Not only that, she watches them humbly follow Him in everyday life. It is hard sometimes because their strong faith makes her family different. Her parents explain to Rachel that following Christ will make her different. It is okay with Rachel because she understands that Jesus was different too.

Rachel's parents often model dependence on God. There aren't any decision this family makes that aren't put in God's hands. And they openly talk about their quest for humility and their battle with pride.

Rachel starts dating a boy from church her senior year. He really pursues her, and she is love-struck. After many months of dates and movies, he wants to take things to the next level. She had always planned on waiting until marriage to have sex, but she loves him. And most of the couples they hang out with, even her Christian friends are already doing it.

Her devotion one night is 1 Thessalonians 5:23.

May God himself, the God of peace, sanctify you through and through.
May your whole spirit, soul and body be kept blameless at the coming of
our Lord Jesus Christ.

After praying about it, she knows what she has to do.

Even though Rachel's boyfriend is from her church youth group, he doesn't act much different than the boys at school. She remembers the "equally yoked" verse (2 Corinthians 6:14), and gets up the courage to break up with him.

She comes home that night heartbroken. Her family smothers her with hugs and kisses. They pray for her that night at dinner. In the evening, her mother stays close by and snuggles with her on the couch. Even in the pain, she feels very loved.

As Rachel's heart begins to heal, she continues to grow in the Lord. She becomes more active in her youth group and is chosen to be a student leader. After going on a mission trip, she feels called to be a missionary.

The following year, Rachel's parents drop her off at a small Christian college several hours from home. After getting her situated in her dorm room, they help her find a local church she can get hooked into. She tries a couple different churches during her four years of college. None of which are quite like the church she grew up in, but she understands the importance of going anyway. Her story of walking with Jesus continues through college and into her adult life.

> *Train up a child in the way he should go, and when he is old*
> *he will not depart from it.*
> Proverbs 22:6 (KJV)

Good Soil

If we had to put our kids into one of these four categories, where would they fall? Our kids may not reject the gospel, but are they passing the tests of faith? They may believe in Jesus, but are they growing spiritually? They may go to church and youth group, but are they bearing fruit in their everyday life?

Most of us go through all four stages in our faith. I have failed a test or two in my journey and been spiritually immature. But I am always growing and learning.

The ground of our youth must be prepared for the seed of the gospel. Just as seeds need the right ingredients to thrive, so does the faith of our kids.

Chapter 4

Why are Our Kids Leaving the Church?
Contributing Factors

"The greatest gift we can give future followers is to recover the imaginative, creative, life that is born through the saving grace of God and hold it out as an invitation to follow."[38]
—Charlie Peacock

There are also many factors that can be toxic to the soil in which the seed is cast. We must protect the environment in which our kids' faith is growing. And we must be their spiritual advocate.

What factors may be contributing to the casual faith of our youth?

Dumbing Down Church

Massive, modern, megachurches have come to define success in the world of Christendom. Gigantic, impressive church buildings on campuses with congregations numbering in the thousands dot the countryside.

I can't tell you how tired I am of hearing the trendy phrase "seeker-friendly." It seems like every church in America has adopted this mantra. The idea is to appeal to the masses. To appeal to the *seeker*. My pastor once called it the "attractional model"—build it, and they will come.

"We have done everything humanly possible to make church "easy." We kept the services short and entertaining, discipleship and evangelism optional, and moral standards low...We figured we could attract more people by offering Jesus with minimal commitment."[39]
–Francis Chan

One might wonder if the goal of the American church has stayed true to God's Word and furthering His Kingdom. Or, has it become a numbers game? Some churches blend into society and culture and bring in the masses. But how far should we go to attract "seekers?"

Seeker-friendly churches are often focused on growth. When churches focus on increasing their numbers, relationships and love become secondary. The concept of unity is often lost in large crowds. And, in a sense, people become numbers.

I recently read a blog post in which the blogger boldly stated that Jesus was *not* seeker-friendly. It made me stop and think. Could this be true?

On the one hand, Jesus spoke in a way that was difficult to understand for those who did not have ears to hear (Matthew 11:15). One could say that He was *not* seeker-friendly. On the other hand, Jesus refers to Himself as the Shepherd who leaves the ninety-nine to find the one lost sheep (Luke 15:4). So, one could also say, that Jesus *was* seeker-friendly.

Either way, we must be careful not to water down the message of the gospel. Regardless of what we want, we need the truth of the gospel, the whole truth. We must also be true to God's main purposes for the church—unity in Christ, fellowship, and love for one another. It's all about relationships.

David Kinnaman writes in his book, *You Lost Me,* "Most young Christians are struggling less with their faith in Christ than with their experience of church."[40]

Has the American church allowed Christianity to become a label instead of a lifestyle? Have we watered down the message of Christ in order to increase our numbers? Would Jesus call our churches "lukewarm?" *Scary thought!*

I know your deeds, that you are neither cold nor hot. I wish you were either
one or the other! So, because you are lukewarm—neither hot nor cold—I
am about to spit you out of my mouth.
Revelation 3:15-16

It is important to examine our churches. To a certain extent, the faith of the youth will reflect the faith of their church.

Church Youth Programs

Jessica, my youngest daughter, recently started guitar lessons. The lessons are at an enormous church in our area in the youth building. Yes, I said youth *building.* They have an entire building just for the youth group.

It is a really cool space, I can't deny it. They call it, "North Beach." I have never seen a youth area quite as impressive and fun as this one. They even have a place where you can get an ice cream cone. It has table games upstairs, lounge areas with comfy couches, a cafe to get your latte, and a huge stage.

Youth rooms, or buildings, these days scream *fun.*

The questions is, are we selling kids entertainment to get them in the doors of our churches? And, once they are in the door, are we showing them a good time or laying out the gospel without any reservations?

Well-known Christian author and lecturer on apologetics, Frank Turek, addresses this issue.

We fail to realize that what we win them with, we win them to. If we win them with entertainment and low commitment, we win them to entertainment and low commitment. Charles Spurgeon was way ahead of his time when he implored the church to start "feeding the sheep rather than amusing the goats."[41]

After we get the youth of our churches in the door, are we giving them sound biblical teaching? Are we focusing on concrete Christian doctrine and Scripture? Is the goal of our youth groups to lead kids to the feet of Jesus? Or, is it to entertain them?

You and I know as parents that it is important to give kids what they need, not just what they want. This principal applies to church youth programs as well. We have to teach the importance of studying Scripture, spending time in prayer, and discipling others. And they need to know what it means to follow Jesus every day.

Let's not forget, however, the primary responsibility of passing on faith to young people lies with the parents, not the youth group leaders, pastors, or ministers. We so often farm out the spiritual formation of our kids to the church. It isn't fair. And it isn't Biblical.

God has tasked *us*, as parents, with training our kids up. Church youth programs and youth leaders exist to support families as they do this.

We don't have to dress Him up; the true person of Jesus Christ, **Himself,** is captivating enough.

We don't have to hide the truth of the gospel. We don't have to constantly impress or entertain our youth. And, we don't need to dress the Savior up in order to make Him more attractive. The true person of Jesus Christ, Himself, is captivating enough. The gospel, in and of itself, is irresistible when it is truly understood.

Intellectual Skepticism and Ignorance of the Faith

In the book, *The Unshakable Truth*, Josh McDowell and Sean McDowell write, "In the recent National Study of Youth and Religion…teenagers were asked, 'Why did you fall away from the faith in which you were raised?' They were given no set of answers to pick from; it was simply an open-ended question. The most common answer—given by thirty-two percent of the respondents—was *intellectual skepticism*."[42]

What is meant by intellectual skepticism and ignorance of the faith? Our kids don't know why they believe in God or why they are a Christian. They don't know why they believe in creation versus evolution. They don't know why they believe the Bible is true. They have just adopted their parents' faith.

There have been times in my life when I wouldn't have known what to say if someone asked me why I believed in God. I would have danced around the question and mostly sounded like I didn't know what I was talking about. Been there, done that. Most of us, if confronted with this question, would probably have a similar response.

Why is the question, *why do you believe in God?* so hard to answer? We may go to church on Sundays, we may do devotionals and Bible studies throughout the week, and we may listen to various teachers of the Word, but many of us still don't know *why* we believe.

How can our kids defend Jesus Christ, on the battlefield of colleges and universities, if they don't even know why they believe in Him? How would they know why they believe in Him if their parents and other Christian adults don't know either? We must do better as a church in our ability to defend our faith. We must lead by example.

We must study basic apologetics. We must have an answer for the *why* questions. And we need to help our kids discover their answers for those questions as well. They are the ones who are likely to be confronted with these issues as they become young men and women.

Our kids are exposed to so much by the time they are eighteen. Sometimes I feel sick to my stomach just thinking about it.

We want our kids to feel confident in their faith and confident that they can handle any challenges they face. We'll talk more about this in Chapter 14.

Feeding Them a Law-Based Faith

Sam Williamson, who writes for *The Noble Heart*, said, "It's virtually one hundred percent predictable that we are converted by one message and then preach another. We are converted by the unbelievable hope of God's love for the undeserving, but we lecture on behavior."[43]

I am so glad there is no condemnation for those who are in Christ Jesus. Praise God! There would be no hope for me if it weren't for grace. I would be hopelessly heading to Hell. And so would you. And, so would our kids. We can't save ourselves from our humanity. We *all* need a Savior.

The story of Jesus' life is about a love so great we can hardly fathom and a pardon so outrageous that none of us deserve.

For sin shall no longer be your master, because you are not
under the law, but under grace.
Romans 6:14

Robin Roberts from the morning show, *Good Morning America,* recently quoted her mother as saying, "God does not love us because of who *we* are, God loves us because of who *He* is." Wow! Right on Robin's Mom!

There isn't anything greater in this world than God's love and grace we have been freely given in Jesus Christ. It's about the *love*, not the *law*. And grace is everything. Let's celebrate that in our homes and in our churches.

For as high as the heavens are above the earth, so great is His love for those
who fear Him; as far as the east is from the west, so far has He removed
our transgressions from us.
Psalm 103:11-12

It is the foolishness and simplicity of the gospel that makes it irresistible. A man died in my place, and therefore, I live. It's lunacy! It's the crazy, radical love that God has for us.

As Christian parents, we seem to focus on what our kids should or shouldn't do when it comes to the faith. I have fallen into this trap myself. Why? Do we focus on the law in our own spiritual walk? I certainly don't.

It's natural for parents to lay down the law. That is what we do. We keep our kids from breaking the law, eating themselves to death, and flunking out of school. They have to follow rules, eat in moderation, *and study, study, study!*

We do this out of love. And we do it because we know what's best for them. However, when it comes to teaching our kids faith, we have to take a different approach.

The girls and I have fought many times about what they are allowed to wear to school. Yoga pants and leggings have been the bane of my existence since they were in middle school! We have struggled and fought with our girls for years about dressing modestly. Modesty is *not* a popular concept.

A couple years ago, they were really into hair, makeup, and fashion. The amount of time and energy they put into her beauty regimen concerned me. I didn't want them to mistakenly think that they were in any way defined by their beauty. Or that beauty can bring them power.

During our devotions one Saturday, I decided to have us study Isaiah 3:16–17.

> *The Lord says, "The women of Zion are haughty, walking along with outstretched necks, flirting with their eyes, strutting along with swaying hips, with ornaments jingling on their ankles. Therefore, the Lord will bring sores on the heads of the women of Zion; the Lord will make their scalps bald."*

The passage goes on to talk about how vain and seductive women can be. It talks about how women use their beauty as a source of power.

You can imagine how well that went over. It was clear what I was doing. *Dumb!* I should have known better.

I came to realize that I was doing the exact thing I am suggesting *not* to do in this book. I was teaching them a law-based faith. I apologized for focusing on the law instead of love and grace.

It's so hard as parents not to make this mistake. What is parenting for in the first decade of our kids' lives if not teaching them right from wrong?

However,

Obedience to Christ must be taught within the context of extreme love and grace.

Kara Powell, coauthor of *Growing Young,* discusses a helpful method for teaching kids faith that avoids the behavior-based model. She takes the basic "guilt—grace—gratitude" model of the Heidelberg Catechism from Reformed theology, and adds the topics, *God's Goodness, God's People* and *God's Vision,* to make it a complete picture of the gospel. She calls it "grounding moral obedience in the invitation of grace."[44]

Guilt is only one small part of the gospel story. We must overwhelm our kids with the message of God's love and grace through the blood of Jesus. And teach them *all* aspects of Christianity.

Powell's method is a great way to teach the gospel to our kids. If we try to keep this progression in mind, they might have a better chance of understanding the true gospel. All aspects of the faith are important. We must not get stuck on guilt and obedience.

He has saved us and called us to a holy life—not because of anything we
have done but because of His own purpose and grace.
2 Timothy 1:9

We must demonstrate the beauty of grace in our parenting. This is crucial. Just as the king forgave the debt of his servant who owed him money in Matthew 18, we must extend grace to our kids. This story shows us if we want God to give us grace, we must offer grace to others.

Young people won't be won to Christ by pounding the rules into their heads. Or, by shaming them. It's our job to teach them about God's abundant love and grace. We must show them the beauty of the gospel.

Feeding Them a Feelings-Based Faith

While we cannot just feed our children the law, we cannot focus solely on feelings either. Nothing about the gospel of Christ tells us that we should focus on our feelings. If we use our feelings as a moral compass, it won't take us long to get way off course.

We have become a "feel good" society. We believe that if we do not feel good or happy, then something must be wrong. Feeling pain or sadness or experiencing suffering of any kind has become unacceptable. We are conditioned to avoid it at all costs.

In his podcast, author, philosopher, Christian theologian, and Christian apologist William Lane Craig defined the "prosperity gospel" as a *betrayal* of the gospel. Nowhere in the Bible does it tell us that if we follow Jesus we will feel good all the time or prosper.

However, according to Scripture, the exact opposite should be true in our lives. If we haven't experienced persecution or suffering as a result of our faith, then there is likely something missing.

In this world you will have trouble.
John 16:33

He doesn't say in this world you *might* have trouble, or in this world *some of you* will have trouble. It is very clear. We *will* have trouble if we follow Him.

> *In fact, everyone who wants to live a godly life in Christ Jesus*
> *will be persecuted.*
> 2 Timothy 3:12

God is Lord over our feelings. He and His Word are trustworthy, while our feelings are not. Our kids our going to learn where to place feelings on the chain of command in their life from looking at us. Therefore, our feelings must be under the obedience of Christ.

> *We demolish arguments and every pretension that sets itself up against the*
> *knowledge of God, and we take captive every thought to make it obedient*
> *to Christ.*
> 2 Corinthians 10:5

We must be careful not to connect faith with feelings when teaching our kids. There are many ways to feel good in this life. If we use faith as a source of good feelings, than faith can easily be replaced with other things; sex, drugs, food, *or cute, fuzzy kittens for that matter!*

We must not point our kids to their feelings as a moral compass. Feelings are unpredictable and unreliable.

> *The heart is deceitful above all things, and desperately sick;*
> *who can understand it?*
> Jeremiah 17: 9

Happiness is not the goal, **holiness** is.

Dysfunction and Divorce

We all know that most families have some degree of dysfunction in them. Just look at any family gathering during the holidays! Families are always going to be imperfect because they are made up of human beings. And as human beings, dysfunction is in our DNA.

In a society where forty-one percent of first marriages and sixty percent of second marriages end in divorce, many kids do not have a stable foundation with which to build.[45] A strong family foundation lays the groundwork for kids to build their own foundation on Jesus Christ.

Divorce is like a nuclear bomb going off in the center of a child's life. I know, I've been there. The effects can be seen far and wide. Ripples of unintended destruction go out from ground zero. Ripples that may not even show up until decades later.

Typically, when a family unit dissolves, inconsistency, insecurity, and instability follow for the children. Their foundation crumbles. Whenever we stray from God's design, chaos and sin are likely to follow. Kids are more likely to flounder when this very foundational element is taken away from them.

Fathers exert a huge impact on their children. Did you know that the word, "father" is found more than eleven hundred times in Scripture? And, "according to the U.S. Census Bureau, twenty-four million children in America—one out of three children—now live in a home in which the biological father is absent.[46]

The role of fathers is significant to the physical, emotional, and spiritual development of kids. God designed fathers to have a special role in raising children—a role only fathers can fill. And their absence can affect a child's view of God.

The National Center for Fathering calls fatherlessness an epidemic.

More than twenty million children live in a home without the physical presence of a father. Millions more have dads who are physically present, but emotionally absent. If it were classified as a disease, fatherlessness would be an epidemic worthy of attention as a national emergency.[47]

They go on to emphasize the seriousness of the situation.

According to 72.2 percent of the U.S. population, fatherlessness is the most significant family or social problem facing America.[48]

Fathers who are absent, abusive, or disinterested also play a role in a child's faith.

Complacent parents also can a have a significant impact on the faith of kids. We all know that the most influential people in your kids' lives are *you*. So, if your faith doesn't appear to be that important to you, than chances are, it is not going to be important to your kids.

Remember when you first accepted Christ? Remember the fire that once burned in you? Where did that passion go? The longer we are Christians and the older we get, the more we have to work at keeping that passion alive.

If there is one thing I have learned in my walk with God, it is that the world is *not* conducive to radically loving Jesus Christ and following him. Nothing about this world, your neighborhood, and maybe even your church will make it easy or comfortable to put God first in your life. There will always be friction. There will always be tension with the world. It will not be easy or natural, but we must be steadfast.

Dysfunction or complacency in families definitely present obstacles for the budding Christian—maybe more so than anything else.

Our second highest priority as Christian parents, after loving our kids, is to help them grow and mature spiritually. As we talked about the parable of the sower in the previous chapter, without maturity, our kids will likely get trampled on, wither away, or get the faith choked out of them. And, many of them will have this fate when they leave our homes.

Seeds need to fall on good soil in order to yield a crop a hundred times more than what was sown. We must be keenly aware of the elements that lead our kids toward or away from a passionate and powerful faith in Christ. We must be discerning about the influences we allow in our kids' lives.

Young people have been leaving the church for decades. This is not a new phenomenon. Christian parents have depended on the church for the spiritual growth of their kids for far too long.

> *"Insanity: Doing the same thing over and over again*
> *but expecting different results"*
> –Albert Einstein

What we are doing is not working if a majority of our kids are leaving the church when they leave our homes. Let's stop the insanity! It is time to try something different.

Part II

A Portrait of Christ

Chapter 5

Are We Different?

Do not conform to the pattern of this world, but be transformed by the
renewing of your mind. Then you will be able to test and approve what
God's will is—his good, pleasing and perfect will.
Romans 12:2

"A world of nice people, content in their own niceness, looking no further,
turned away from God, would be just as desperately in need of salvation as
a miserable world and might even be more difficult to save."[49]
—C.S. Lewis

In 1993, Phil Vischer created VeggieTales, a series of children's videos teaching Bible stories. My girls loved them when they were little. And to this day, sometimes in church when the pastor is preaching on a story from the Bible, all I can think about is Bob, the Tomato, and Larry, the Cucumber.

In a sermon series on Daniel, my pastor recently talked about the story of Shadrach, Meshach, and Abednego and the fiery furnace. As much as I tried to pay attention, all I could think about was Veggie Tales's and the "The Bunny Song."

> *The Bunny, the bunny, whoa I love the bunny.*
> *I don't love my mom or my dad, just the bunny.*

This is a song from a VeggieTales video, *Rack, Shack & Benny,* that tells a story about Nebby K. Nezzer, who runs a chocolate bunny factory. He makes a giant chocolate bunny that he commands all his workers to bow down and worship.

Someday when I'm old, I may not remember who I am, but I will remember the lyrics to these songs!

All Except Three

Four young boys—Daniel, Shadrach, Meshach, and Abednego—in the book of Daniel, are brought to the palace to be groomed to serve the king. Imagine being taken from your home and family as a young boy. How frightening that must have been.

It is quickly apparent that they far outshine all the other boys brought to the palace in wisdom and understanding. They are even found greater than all the magicians and astrologers in the kingdom. So they are put in charge of Babylon, "one of the most pagan civilizations in human history."[50]

Shadrach, Meshach and Abednego were just trying to mind their own business and do their job when they were asked to bow down to a gold statue built by King Nebuchadnezzar in Daniel 3. The stand they took was extraordinarily brave and put their lives in great danger.

Picture administrators, governors, counselors, treasurers, judges, magistrates, and all the officials of the provinces gathered in front of the golden image that King Nebuchadnezzar had set up.

And all the people bowed down. All except three.

Only the sound of the warm, wind whipping through the air breaks the silence. The whole kingdom is bowing down before the golden image.

Nebuchadnezzar's men look out over the bowing masses. Wait…*what is that?* They say, squinting to see. It's so far away, the image is fuzzy. Could there be men who are standing? Do they not know what their fate will be if they disobey the king?

> *Furious with rage, Nebuchadnezzar summoned Shadrach, Meshach and Abednego. So these men were brought before the king, and Nebuchadnezzar said to them, "Is it true, Shadrach, Meshach and Abednego, that you do not serve my gods or worship the image of gold I have set up?…if you do not worship it, you will be thrown immediately into a blazing furnace. Then what god will be able to rescue you from my hand?"*
> Daniel 3:13-15

Their reply to the king is simple, but profound. Oh, if I only had faith as great!

> *Shadrach, Meshach and Abednego replied to him, "King Nebuchadnezzar, we do not need to defend ourselves before you in this matter. If we are thrown into the blazing furnace, the God we serve is able to deliver us from it, and he will deliver us from Your Majesty's hand. But even if he does not, we want you to know, Your Majesty, that we will not serve your gods or worship the image of gold you have set up."*
> Daniel 3:16-18

Wow. What courage they had. Even in the face of death.

Are we willing to be the "all except three?" Are we willing to be the exception in our communities? Are we willing to be different and stand out as we stand up for Christ?

If we are not different than the world, then we are not just *in* it, we are *of* it.

An Honest Look

Kids must see their parents as different—different than people of other faiths and different than people who have no faith. Parents need to model generosity, faithfulness, and complete trust in God.

Our kids will take faith seriously when they see **us** take it seriously.

Dallas Willard writes in his book, *The Great Omission*, "the word "disciple" occurs 269 times in the New Testament. "Christian" is found only three times and was first introduced to refer precisely to disciples of Jesus."[51]

Today, very few of us think of ourselves as *disciples*. And even the word, *Christian*, has lost its meaning.

> *"There is an obvious great disparity between, on the one hand, the hope for life expressed in Jesus…and, on the other hand, the actual day-to-day behavior, inner life, and social presence of most of those who now profess adherence to him."*[52]
> –Dallas Willard, *The Great Omission*

Just because I am a woman, and I have faith, does not mean that I am a woman who lives by faith. Just because a person believes in God and is a man, does not make him a Godly man. What we seek to be as Christian parents are Godly men and women.

David Kinnaman and Gabe Lyons identify a couple different types of Christians in their book, *Good Faith. Legacy* Christians are those who identify with Christianity but don't prioritize their faith.[53] The majority of Americans fall in this category. They are CINOs—*Christians in name only*. And, "three in five American Christians are mostly inactive in their faith."[54]

*"We're Protestants, we just try to obey the commandments
and keep our heads down."*
—Mike Heck from the TV series, *The Middle*

Then there are *practicing* Christians who attend church on a regular basis and consider their faith a priority.[55] Those in this camp consider Christianity a lifestyle not just a label. "Three out of ten are practicing Christians."[56]

Practicing Christians believe that God sent His one and only Son Jesus Christ to die for the sins of the world. They know the gospel and have heard the message many times. Their faith is an important part of their life. They go to church on Sundays, celebrate religious holidays, and listen to the pastor to learn about God. Practicing Christians seek to pass down the tradition of church to their kids.

However, I would add a third type of follower of Christ called *disciples.*

Disciples radically follow the teaching of Christ. They recognize the importance of reading and studying Scripture and pray often. God isn't a part of their life, He is their *whole* life. They realize they are sinners and understand their need for a Savior. Community in the body of Christ is important to them, and they therefore gather together with other disciples to pray and encourage each other in boldness. Disciples actively seek God's will and make it their mission to go out and make disciples.

If we long to be disciples, we must be different.

Therefore, come out from them and be separate, says the Lord.
2 Corinthians 6:17

There are key issues that disciples of Christ need to handle differently than the world. The possibility of persecution, tension with the culture, church, and our lifestyle/traditions are some of them.

Persecution and Suffering

When Jesus appointed seventy-two followers to go before Him to every town in Luke 10, He warned them.

Go! I am sending you out like lambs among wolves.
Luke 10:3

The image of lambs among wolves gives us a very graphic picture of ripping and tearing of flesh. Doesn't sound pleasant, does it?

Persecution is so far from our understanding as Americans. We figure, because we live in America, we are immune to it. *Not true.*

Christ tells us to take up our cross and follow Him. We can assume that if our worst cross to bear is getting stuck in traffic, getting the wrong drink at Starbucks, or losing our wifi, than we are missing the mark. Taking up your cross is not referring to first world problems. Crosses are heavy, burdensome, and painful, not simply inconvenient.

Does living a Christian life require suffering or persecution? What if someone hasn't experienced a tragedy, trauma, or a major trial in their life? Does this mean they are doing something wrong?

While it may be true that some people are luckier than others in their circumstances in life, we all must take up our cross and follow Him. There is no other way.

*Learn to do right; seek justice. Defend the oppressed. Take up the cause of
the fatherless; plead the case of the widow.*
Isaiah 1:17

One could say that we invite suffering when we defend the oppressed, take up the cause of the fatherless, or plead the case of the widow. Feeding the poor, attending to the sick, and taking the gospel to the farthest corners of the world will likely lead to suffering or persecution.

If we are doing these things, we will not lead a suffering-free life.

Living in America does not excuse us from what Christ commands us to do. We must feed the hungry, invite in the lonely, clothe those in need, look after the sick, and visit those in prison.

All of us must step out of our comfort zone and consider the following:

- *going into areas where people are in need (ie. third world countries or the inner city)*
- *inviting in the outcasts (give attention and care to those who are outside of our circle)*
- *giving away our things to people who need them more (sacrifice enough money so that it hurts a little; don't just give out of our excess)*
- *visiting prisons (go to places where you don't feel comfortable and you may not be safe)*
- *adopting an orphan (open your home to someone who doesn't have one)*

Does living the life of a disciple require suffering? Absolutely, it does.

It requires sacrifice and discomfort and *suffering*. If we are in God's Word and doing what Scripture says, then we may find ourselves in scary, uncomfortable, and even dangerous places attending to the needy and sick.

Tension with the Culture

"When we look at the broadest segment of practicing Christians…a majority says they feel misunderstood and persecuted, while millions of others use terms like marginalized, sidelined, silenced, afraid to speak up, and afraid to look stupid."[57]
–David Kinnaman and Gabe Lyons, *Good Faith*

As a Christian, how do you feel in the culture around you? Misunderstood? Persecuted? Marginalized? Sidelined? Are you afraid to speak up or afraid to look stupid? We all have been at one time or another. Disciples of Christ experience these things. They don't quite fit in, they are counterculture.

Whenever our life is in alignment with the culture, whenever we fit in with society, whenever our life is going along smoothly, we need to assume something is *wrong,* not right.

Pastor and author Joel Osteen urges Christians to claim their prosperity. "God wants us to prosper financially, to have plenty of money, to fulfill the destiny He has laid out for us." He says. Don't believe it. God wants you to be more like *Him*. Period.

The prosperity gospel is one of the biggest lies of our time.

If we are seeking righteousness and following Jesus, we may not prosper, we may not be financially stable, and we may not be healed, but we certainly will feel tension with the culture—just as Jesus did.

When Christ talked about things like loving your enemies, turning the other cheek, and selling all that you have and giving it to the poor, it caused "tension with the culture." Preaching that we were all equal in God's eyes created "tension with the culture." And proclaiming the coming of the Kingdom of God created "tension with the culture."

I would say that one could sum up Jesus ministry on earth as "tension with the culture." This was ultimately lived out in the cry for His death.

"What shall I do, then, with the one you call the king of the Jews?" Pilate asked them. "Crucify him!" they shouted.
Mark 15:12-13

The early church experienced tension with the culture. Tension because they were doing things differently. And tension because their loyalty was to the risen Jesus and no longer to the rulers of the day.

We must ask ourselves, *when is the last time I felt tension with the culture?*

Holidays

As I put our pumpkin away after Halloween last year, I thought about all the money that we spend on holidays in this country. It was estimated that Americans would spend $8.4 billion dollars in 2016 on Halloween.[58]

According to figures derived from a national survey completed by Prosper Insights & Analytics, "the average consumer plans to spend $935.58 on all things Christmas, Hanukkah and Kwanzaa this year (2016)."[59]

The 2016 Deloitte Holiday Survey reported even more shocking numbers.

"The total expected holiday (Christmas) sales this year are actually expected to exceed one trillion."[60]

Wow! One *TRILLION* dollars! Mind. Blown.

We spend so much money for one day on the calendar when according to a Pew Research Center report, seventy-one percent of the world's population lives off of ten dollars a day.[61] Nearly half of the world's population—more than three billion people—live on less than $2.50 a day. And more than 1.3 billion people live in extreme poverty—less than $1.25 a day. Right now, one billion children worldwide are living in poverty. And according to UNICEF, twenty-two thousand children who live in poverty die each day.[62]

If the three billion people in the world who make less than $2.50 a day work every single day for a year, they earn less than $912.50 a year. We, in this country, spend almost that same amount of money for *one* day.

Christmas is the story of Jesus coming to the world to save us. He was a King, yet His crown was made of thorns, not adorned with jewels. And Jesus came with a message of hope and peace. He taught us to love our enemies, take care of the poor, and turn the other cheek. He taught us to focus our attention outward, on others.

Yet often, at Christmas time, we send the message to our kids that causes them to focus inward, to focus on "self." The message of Santa Claus is to focus on *me*. What do *I* want for Christmas? How many presents will *I* get this year?

What if we had never introduced Santa Claus, Rudolph the Red-Nosed Reindeer, or Frosty the Snowman? What if our observance of Christmas had always been about the message of Christ? What if we taught our kids *selflessness* at Christmastime? What if they saw us, their parents, giving generously to the poor instead of to them for Christmas? What might they learn from that?

As I write this, *A Charlie Brown Christmas* is on TV. The message of Charles Schulz in this show is brilliant. He saw the materialism and all the silly things we focus on during the Christmas season back in 1965. He tried to portray the true meaning of the birth of Christ, and show us how we have strayed from it.

Schulz illustrated beautifully how we were, and still are, valuing the wrong things at Christmas. *The money, the stuff, and the lights…oh my!*

Charlie Brown: *"I am in sad shape."*

Lucy: *"Wait a minute, before you begin I must ask that you pay in advance. five cents please."* (Charlie Brown puts a nickel in the can)

Lucy: *"Boy what a sound! How I love hearing that old money plink! That beautiful sound of cold, hard, cash! That beautiful, beautiful sound! Nickles, nickles, nickles! That beautiful sound of plinking nickles!"*

How we handle Christmas speaks volumes to our kids about our faith. What is most important in our family at Christmas time? Jesus. It's all about Jesus.

The story of Christ's birth has very little to do with family. In fact, when Jesus was immaculately conceived, Mary and Joseph were not yet married.

Christ's birth has everything to do with God and His amazing love for us. Christmas is about one person—*Jesus Christ*. It's not about you and it's not about me. And our kids need to learn that it's not about them either.

Christmas is the beginning of the greatest love story that ever was or ever could be. It is about our transformation from being condemned in the flesh to being redeemed in the blood of Jesus. Are we responding appropriately to this amazing gift?

I so often find myself spending money that I don't have at Christmas on things that people don't really want or need or could easily buy themselves.

We build up the idol of Christmas and shrink Jesus in the process. What does *Jesus* actually want from us?

For I was hungry and you gave me something to eat, I was thirsty and you gave me something to drink, I was a stranger and you invited me in, I needed clothes and you clothed me, I was sick and you looked after me, I was in prison and you came to visit me... Truly I tell you, whatever you did for one of the least of these brothers and sisters of mine, you did for me.
Matthew 25:35-36,40

Most of our moms and dads, brothers and sisters, and aunts and uncles are not the "least of these." Why are we spending our time and money giving things to each other at Christmas? How can we be so focused on ourselves and our families when half of the world's population lives in poverty?

It doesn't make any sense.

I can't think of the last time that I was starving, because I never have been. I can't imagine being sick and not being able to just go to the drug store, or a doctor's office, or the hospital. And I wake up every day in my sixty-eight degree bedroom and get up out of my sleep number bed. I live in a house that has way more space than we'll ever need. And my refrigerator and pantry are full of food.

I don't have to get wet when it rains, be cold on blustery winter days, or sweat in the extreme heat of summer. I don't ever have to hunger or thirst. Every single physical need you and I have is met.

We, as Americans, are the greatest, not the least. Therefore, we have a great responsibility to care for those less fortunate than us.

If anyone has material possessions and sees a brother or sister in need but has no pity on them, how can the love of God be in that person?
1 John 3:17

We must live differently, even during the holidays.

What if we viewed Christmas in light of eternity? What if we looked at it in the context of the Scripture that tells us to store up treasures in Heaven (Matthew 6:20)? Would we do anything differently?

It all comes down to this question: Do I want to receive my reward in full in this life, or do I want to wait and enjoy my reward eternally in heaven? When we look at it this way, it's a no brainer. If we delay our gratification there is a huge payoff. And the payoff is guaranteed. We all die eventually.

"He is no fool who gives what he cannot keep to gain what he cannot lose."
—Jim Elliot

Are we willing to give up a little of what we love so much about Christmas to store up treasures in heaven?

The holidays usually consists of,

- *shopping for gifts.*
- *decorating our homes.*
- *giving and receiving presents.*
- *throwing parties.*
- *eating Christmas cookies.*
- *spending time with family.*

None of these things are bad.

But, why would we forfeit eternal treasures for *just* these things? Eternity with God in heaven will probably have these wonderful things and a thousand times more! And we will get to keep them forever!

What I am saying is we need to help the poor and serve others. We must focus on blessing others more than we expect to be blessed ourselves. Not only because Christ commands it, but also because Christ will *reward* it.

If we are celebrating Christ's birth, how can we celebrate it any other way than to "do unto the least of these?"

In everything I did, I showed you that by this kind of hard work we must help the weak, remembering the words the Lord Jesus Himself said: "It is more blessed to give than to receive."
Acts 20:35

If we are serving the poor and oppressed, we can still enjoy some Christmassy things while at the same time being expectant of our future treasure. But when we skip over the commandments of Jesus to celebrate Christmas "our way," we are being "of" the world not just "in" it.

Christmas can be a huge distraction from the mission of furthering His Kingdom. If you are like me, it doesn't take much to succumb to distraction. Wave shiny objects in front of me and I am gone...*squirrel!* So, we must see beyond the lights and the tinsel. Our focus must remain on Christ and His mission even during the Christmas season.

The Son of Man did not come to be served, but to serve, and to give His life as a ransom for many.
Matthew 20:28

As disciples of Christ, we put Him above everything else. And putting Christ above everything requires that we put others above ourselves.

This year as the holidays come and go, how can we store up treasures in heaven with our money, time, and talents?

- *What if we gave all of our gifts to people that we will never even meet?*
- *What if we gave gifts to orphaned children halfway across the world?*
- *What if we gave it all to the downcast and lowly?*

Or, try giving a portion of what you normally spend on each other for Christmas to the homeless in your city—just a portion. See how God blesses you, and then, next year give a little more.

Spend part of your holiday handing out food at a bread pantry. Invite an elderly neighbor, or someone who doesn't have family over for Christmas. Hand out blankets to the homeless. Give money to the bell ringers for The Salvation Army outside of the grocery store every time you encounter them. Tip waiters and waitresses double what you usually tip. These are all things you can do at Christmas to honor Christ.

———————

According to David Kinnaman and Gabe Lyons, we are counterculture when we:

- *Love others well*
- *Remain committed to orthodox beliefs*
- *Make space for those who disagree*
- *Stand out from the crowd*
- *Ask the right questions*
- *Live under God's moral order*
- *Offer a vision of human intimacy beyond sex*
- *Practice hospitality*
- *Do the good, hard work of racial reconciliation*
- *Value human life, in every form, at every stage*
- *Love our gay friends and trust God's design for sex*
- *Build households of faith*
- *Are theologically grounded and culturally responsive*
- *Make disciples*
- *Practice the sacred art of seeing people*
- *Make disciples and faith communities that are Christ like*[63]

If we are not different than the non-believing community around us, then we are not living the life of a disciple of Christ. Either we are living for God, or we're not. There is no halfway.

Following Christ is a full-time gig. If we are not living radically for Him, then what are we doing? Why are we going to our churches? Why are we singing our praise songs? Why do we call ourselves Christians at all?

"Something is wrong when our lives make sense to unbelievers."
–Francis Chan, *Crazy Love*

God doesn't just want our tithes and offerings, our prayers and songs, and our time and talents. He wants us to give Him *everything*. Once we give Him everything, we are never the same.

Jesus answered, "If you want to be perfect, go, sell your possessions and give to the poor, and you will have treasure in heaven. Then come, follow me."
Matthew 19:21

The amount of love and grace that God gives us is unfathomable. He gives us life when we deserve death. How can we not give Him everything?

God, I pray, make me better than I am without You. Please make me more like You. I give everything to You, Abba Father, because You are everything. Teach me to be humble and live a life of simplicity. Help me to separate myself from the materialistic things of this world. Change my nature to be more like Yours. When people look at me, I want them to see You, Jesus.

Chapter 6

Three Elements of a Contagious Faith: First, Love

"Sadly, many young people do not have a sense of vocation because millions of Christian parents have a vision of following Jesus that avoids anything more demanding than faithful church attendance. Our children can't catch what we don't already have."[64]
–David Kinnaman, *You Lost Me*

On a mission, I grabbed the Clorox wipes and hurried to the kitchen. In my mind, all I could see was a teeming cesspool of germs. My daughter had just gotten over the flu and strep. So, I wiped down the refrigerator handles, the microwave, the faucets, door handles, and the knobs on the stove. I wanted to bomb the place with Lysol.

This winter has been rough in our household. We couldn't stay well. Thank goodness for the MinuteClinic! *In-out-on antibiotics-and back to bed! And just my style…no doctors!*

We try not to pass it to each other, but we almost always do.

Just like those pesky germs, our character, *who we are*, is likely to be contagious as well. Contagious to those around us, and contagious to our kids.

Let's face it, we all catch ourselves mimicking things our parents used to say from time to time. Why? Our behavior and character are contagious. And if we are living a life of obedience to Christ, our faith will be contagious as well.

We, as Christian parents, are the first step in the equation of our kids' faith. Whether our kids develop a personal and passionate faith, or a casual, watered down faith, depends a great deal on the faith and character of Mom and Dad.

If we long to reflect the image of Jesus to our kids, we must show fruit in our character.

> *But the fruit of the Spirit is love, joy, peace, forbearance, kindness, goodness, faithfulness, gentleness, and self-control.*
> Galatians 5:22-23

Jesus modeled all of these characteristics. However, there are three overarching themes in the character of Christ, under which everything else falls. Three characteristics define the life of Jesus. These are the three things teenagers need to see in their parents if their faith is going to be contagious.

First, Love

In 2001, Steven Spielberg came out with an extraordinary movie called *A.I. Artificial Intelligence*, exploring the question, *how far would someone go to be loved?*

In this heart-wrenching tale of a boy's desire to be loved, Haley Joel Osment plays a robot boy named David, who goes to great lengths to earn back the love of, who he believes is, his mother. He goes to the ends of the earth and spends thousands of years looking for the blue fairy that will make him a "real boy" so his mom will love him.

Even though he is a robot, it is an excellent depiction of the lengths that one will go to for love. It is the human condition. We desperately desire to be loved.

Loving with a deep, abiding love comes not from ourselves, but from the realm of the divine.

The first element of a contagious faith is *love*. Kids must see that their parents love well.

God preceded everything. And love began with Him. God *is* love and without *Him*, our world would be devoid of it.

The most important characteristic we must possess to show our kids the person of Jesus is *love*. God loved us first. And His love has gone above and beyond what we could ever desire or imagine.

God didn't just love the world, He so loved the world. (John 3:16) God doesn't just want us to have life, He wants us to have it abundantly. (John 10:10) God doesn't just love us in this lifetime, His love endures forever (Psalm 136).

This is the message we need to teach our kids every day. We need to pour God's love into our kids. We must pour it in until their cup overflows.

Dear friends, let us love one another, for love comes from God. Everyone who loves has been born of God and knows God. Whoever does not love does not know God, because God is love.
1 John 4:7-8

As love flows in from God, love must also go out from us in three directions. First, love must go up.

If someone asked you if you loved God, you would probably say, *yes*. We all would. But what does it really mean to love God? Love is not a feeling or a fact. As DC Talk sang back in the 90s, "Luv is a Verb."

We were put on this earth to love. As disciples of Christ, we must actively, willfully, deliberately, intentionally, and fully love God and His Son, Jesus Christ above all else. Loving God and bringing *Him* glory should be the first thing we do.

> *Love the Lord your God with all your heart and with all your soul and with all your mind and with all your strength.*
> Mark 12:30

I have been a Christian for a long time, and I know this verse well. I've heard and read it many times. Loving God seems so elementary. But the worst thing we could do is take loving Him for granted.

> *Remember your Creator in the days of your youth, before the days of trouble come and the years approach when you will say,*
> *"I find no pleasure in them."*
> Ecclesiastes 12:1

It is tempting to focusing on the second commandment to love your neighbor, first. However, we cannot bypass the *Love the Lord your God* and be fruitful in ministry. *Love your neighbor as yourself* is not the most important commandment. Loving *Him* is.

Our attention is so easily swayed to the *to do* list of Christianity. Tasks clutter our mind and leave little room for focusing on God Himself. Does this sound familiar?

> ✓ *Did I pray today?*
> ✓ *Did I read my bible today?*
> ✓ *Did I serve others today?*

Our focus must not be on the *doing*, but on the *loving*. The doing comes out of the loving. Just as the fruits of the spirit come from spending time with God and studying His Word.

We have fit God neatly into our daily planners. God doesn't want to be something that we just check off of our lists. He wants to be known, pursued, experienced, and adored with the intensity and desperation of David or Job. He wants to be loved to the fullest expression.

No one loved God like David did. This was a man after God's own heart.

I love the Lord, for He heard my voice; He heard my cry for mercy. Because
He turned His ear to me, I will call on Him as long as I live.
Psalm 116:1-2

We are incapable of loving God the way He deserves to be loved without His help. After all, God created the heavens and the earth. He breathed massive stars into being. And He is omniscient, omnipotent, and omnipresent. Therefore, how can I, such a small, insignificant being, love Him—*and love Him well?*

Author and speaker, Francis Chan, addresses this in his book, *Crazy Love*.

The fact is, I need God to help me love God…Something mysterious, even supernatural must happen in order for genuine love for God to grow in our hearts. The Holy Spirit has to move in our lives. It is a remarkable cycle: Our prayers for more love result in love, which naturally causes us to pray more, which results in more love…[65]

If we ask God every day to increase our love for Him, and if our eyes are continually on God, then our love for Him will grow.

We are told to love God with all of our hearts and souls. We need to constantly be evaluating where our treasure is. Our treasure lies where we spend our time and money. Our treasure is what we spend our mental energy on. Our treasure is what we most highly value.

Our lifestyle is a dead give-away of where our heart truly is.

We are also told in Scripture to love God with all of our mind.

My brother Greg is a smart guy. One could say he is an intellectual. He loves identifying stars and constellations, listening to debates, and reading *really* long, scholarly books. When he goes to a museum, he's the guy who reads everything. I mean *everything*!

Greg feels closest to God when he is discovering or learning.

Most of us have questions for God. Things we want to know and understand. Things that frustrate us. *Will we know everything in heaven? Will we get all the answers to life's questions when we get there?*

Greg once commented about these questions.

> When we reach heaven, one of two things will happen: either our minds will be co-equal with God, or we will be forever learning. Since I do not believe that our minds could ever be capable of omniscience, I believe that we will forever be learning about God and His created order. And I wouldn't have it any other way!

He wants to spend eternity exploring and learning new things. He finds great joy in discovering the mysteries about science and nature and he hopes that will continue in heaven. He is loving God with all of his *mind*.

How else can we love God with our mind?

Study apologetics. Learn how the physical universe points to our Creator. Study the arguments for creation versus evolution. Look at all the evidence that points to the truth of the resurrection. Studying these things help us to know God more. And *knowing* Him more causes us to *love* Him more.

I was blown away by a sermon given by Louie Giglio at a conference in which he talked about *laminin*.

> Laminin is a protein that is part of the extracellular matrix in humans and animals…Laminin and other ECM proteins essentially "glue" the cells (such as those in the lining of the stomach and

intestines) to a foundation of connective tissue. This keeps the cells in place and allows them to function properly.[66]

Basically, laminin is a protein that holds our bodies together. And this protein molecule is in the shape of the cross of our Lord Jesus Christ! Go ahead, Google it! It'll knock your socks off! There is no limit to the imprint of God on His creation.

I am fascinated by these crazy, random facts about God's creation. It increases my love for and awe of Him. Maybe the only reason he made laminin the way he did was to remind us of His great love for us.

So much of the time, however, we are spiritually lazy when it comes to loving God with our minds. We tend to love God with our heart, our soul, and our emotions, but not necessarily our intellect. Our minds are sort of "off limits." But why? If we are to be *"a living sacrifice, holy and pleasing to God" (Romans 12:1)* then we must not hold anything back from Him.

It's not okay for us to neglect to love God with our intellect. Who created quantum physics, molecular biology, complex molecules, nebulae and pulsars, solar flares, gamma rays, theology, philosophy, and everything in history? God did. And we should seek to grow *intellectually* in our faith. After all, why would God give us such a sophisticated brain if He didn't want us to use it for *His* glory?

While you may not consider yourself an intellectual, challenge yourself to learn something new about the world. You might be surprised by how interesting God's creation really is. Discovery, in and of itself, is a gift from God. And it might absolutely light you up if you give it a chance.

Spending time in Scripture is another way to love God with our minds. Pondering the things of God and His Word can be the greatest time of revelation. And greater understanding of our Creator, Savior, Redeemer, and God leads to greater love.

You will keep in perfect peace those whose minds are steadfast,
because they trust in you
Isaiah 26:3

Everything in our being exists to love God and bring *Him* glory.

Loving God with all of our strength means keeping our bodies strong and healthy. We are told in Scripture that our bodies are not our own. They are a temple for the Lord.

> *Do you not know that your bodies are temples of the Holy Spirit, who is in*
> *you, whom you have received from God? You are not your own.*
> 1 Corinthians 6:19

Exercise and athleticism can be an act of worship. When teams pray before a game, it is an act of worship.

We also need to love the Lord with our actions. When we obey His Word and His laws, we are loving Him.

> *He has shown you, O mortal, what is good. And what does the Lord*
> *require of you? To act justly and to love mercy and to walk humbly with*
> *your God.*
> Micah 6:8

Michael Smalley posed this question on a Sunday morning at our church a couple months ago. "What was Jesus' love language?" I had never thought of Jesus having a love language.

In Gary Chapman's 1995 book, *The Five Love Languages*, he identified the five love languages as, words of affirmation, quality time, receiving gifts, acts of service, and physical touch.[67]

What was Jesus' love language? I repeated in my head. I figured it was a trick question. *All of them?* I supposed. He went on to say that Jesus' love language was obedience. Of course!

> *If you love me, obey my commands...Whoever has my commands and*
> *keeps them is the one who loves me.*
> John 14:15,21

Our kids will see that we love Jesus if we obey his commands.

I love the story in Scripture where Jesus asks Peter three times if he loves Him (John 21:15-17). Not only does Jesus give Him a chance to redeem himself from denying Him three times (Luke 22:54-60), but it is also a profound teaching moment.

I can almost hear Jesus saying, "OK, now that we are past that, let me teach you what it means to love me…"

And finally, in order to actively love God, we must be in *relationship* with Him. Relationship indicates an ongoing and active connection. If I loved my husband, but never talked to him or spent time with him, we would have a problem. God wants to know that we love him and desire a relationship with Him.

I am the vine; you are the branches. If you remain in me and I in you, you will bear much fruit; apart from me you can do nothing.
John 15:5

"The love Jesus longs for is not just devotion. It's also emotion. It's not just volition. It is also affection. It is not just discipline. It is also passion. It's not just routine. It is also romance."[68]
–Beth Moore, *Audacious*

Idols

If we are not loving God first, then we have idols.

You shall have no other gods before me.
Exodus 20:3

We so easily fall into having idols without even realizing it. We would never claim that we put anything before God, but most of us probably do. We must examine our daily life if we are to discover the truth.

- *how much time do we spend with God?*
- *how much time do we spend with family?*
- *how much time do we spend focusing on our spouse?*
- *how much money do we spend on ourselves?*
- *how much of our life resembles the life of Christ?*

These questions help us take an honest look at ourselves. God does not tolerate idols.

According to author and speaker Francis Chan, "how we spend our time, what our money goes toward, and where we will invest our energy is equivalent to choosing God or rejecting Him."[69]

If we teach our kids that anything is more important than God, than we are teaching them to have idols. And kids learn by what we do, not as much by what we say. God must be first in our lives. Seek *first* the Kingdom of God.

But seek first his kingdom and his righteousness, and all these things will be given to you as well.
Matthew 6:33

Our focus must be on the Creator, not the creation, on the Healer, not the healing, on the Provider, not the provision, and on the Great I AM who blesses, not the blessing.

Love goes upward first. Loving God is number one.

We must also send love downward, to our kids. How we love our kids will be a powerful witness as to how we love. Our kids need great amounts of love, especially if they are to become adults who love much. We must constantly be pouring into them.

And finally, love must go outward. Often, the most powerful expression of love is when and how we love "our neighbor." Our kids must see us love others. And not just those who are easy to love—even the prickly ones.

I have been mentoring a young woman who, until a couple years ago, was homeless in the inner city. She has four kids, ages three and under.

On my way to picking her up every time, I pray that God would increase my love for her. I want to walk alongside her and love her well. But without God, I am incapable of such love. The struggle within me to love her is real.

God really convicted me in this relationship. My job is not to *fix* her, my job is to *love* her. We cannot love others well when we have an agenda. We must surrender our will to the will of God in our relationships. Only then can we love our neighbors well.

If we try to fix people or serve them without love, we are like a clanging symbol.

If I speak in the tongues of men or of angels, but do not have love, I am only a resounding gong or a clanging cymbal.
1 Corinthians 13:1

Chapter 7

Three Elements of a Contagious Faith: Second, Humility

"The point is, He wants you to know Him: wants to give you Himself. And, He and you are two things of such a kind that if you really get into any kind of touch with Him you will, in fact, be humble - delightedly humble, feeling the infinite relief of having for once got rid of all the silly nonsense about your own dignity which has made you restless and unhappy all of your life."[70]
—C.S. Lewis, *Mere Christianity*

Jesus was loving, powerful, merciful, gracious, gentle, kind, and so much more. Among the many wonderful characteristics that He exhibited was humility. This is the most striking and beautiful description of Jesus. He was the perfect picture of a servant king.

The Son of Man did not come to be served, but to serve, and to give his life
as a ransom for many.
Matthew 20:28

There is nothing that makes Christianity more attractive than a display of humility in a Christian.

In order to address the topic of humility, we must first address our pride. Pride is in our nature, humility takes work.

The Greatest Sin

Pride is at my doorstep and lurking around every corner. It is just waiting to spring out of me like a wretched weed. I am constantly in battle. Who will win today? God or Pride? Daily, I sway back and forth between insecurity and overconfidence; and between humility and pride. Rarely do I hit that sweet spot of exactly where God wants me to be.

As I claw my way to a life completely dependent on God, I long for more of *Him* and less of me.

My favorite movie of all time is *Independence Day*. Humor, aliens, Will Smith…the perfect ingredients for an all time classic!

Whenever I think of having more of God and less of me, I think of a scene from this movie. Huge spaceships are breaking through earth's atmosphere and positioning themselves all over the world. One is approaching airspace over a naval submarine in the Pacific ocean. The gargantuan spacecraft overtakes the airspace above, and is so massive that the entire radar fills with red. From top to bottom it goes until it is completely consumed. That is what I visualize when I think of God consuming me. I don't want him to be a couple of dots on my radar. I need Him to fill the whole thing!

He must become greater; I must become less.
John 3:30

Pride is anything that turns our focus inward, on ourselves, instead of on God.

Pride has never been explained more eloquently than in the chapter entitled, "The Greatest Sin" in C.S. Lewis's book, *Mere Christianity*.

> The essential vice, the utmost evil, is Pride. Unchastity, anger, greed, drunkenness, and all that, are mere flea bites in comparison: it was through Pride that the devil became the devil: Pride leads to every other vice: it is the complete anti-God state of mind.[71]

All of us at one time or another will struggle with pride. And, most of us will struggle with it every day. It is Satan's greatest tool.

> *Before his downfall a man's heart is proud.*
> Proverbs 18:12 (HCSB)

> *"Faith that grows proud ceases to be faith. It begins to be a god...Satan has a way to counterfeit every genuine attempt to obey God."[72]*
> –Beth Moore, *Believing God*

I love the boldness of Paul. He had Godly wisdom and a strong faith. He probably dealt with pride on a daily basis. And, God dealt with Paul about his pride as well.

> *Therefore, in order to keep me from becoming conceited, I was given a thorn in my flesh, a messenger of Satan, to torment me. Three times I pleaded with the Lord to take it away from me. But He said to me, "My grace is sufficient for you, for My power is made perfect in weakness."*
> 2 Corinthians 12:7-9

Acknowledging weakness is the posture of bowing to the Lord and acknowledging His sovereignty. Recognizing our weakness is recognizing our place *beneath* our Almighty God. This requires that we put down our pride.

We aren't letting God work fully in us when we are filled with pride. The Holy Spirit and pride cannot occupy the same space. We must choose if we are going to be led by the Spirit in humility or driven by pride. It's one or the other.

When we move in **God's** power, **He** is glorified.
When we move in our own power, **we** are glorified.

"Reliance on ourselves is no option in light of the cross. However fantastically marvelous we may think we are, the cross is God's verdict on us as sinners. It annihilates even the possibility of finally placing our trust in ourselves."[73]
–Michael Reeves, *Rejoicing in Christ*

Most of us don't seem that concerned with pride. It just isn't on our radar. One of the greatest victories over Satan that we can have is constant awareness and repentance of our pride. If we do this, Satan loses his power.

I've had my share of hard knocks in life. From difficulty and strife grows the fruit of wisdom. It's a gift from God because He uses all things for good. And, He rewards those who persevere. But...*look out!* How easily pride can grow out of one's wisdom and strength like a fungus.

Your heart will become proud and you will forget the Lord your God.
Deuteronomy 8:14

"God wants to bear much fruit in every one of our lives. He wants to infuse our prayer lives with inconceivable power...but He will not tolerate any of our attempts to share His glory."[74]
–Beth Moore, *Believing God*

To think that we can do it better than the Creator of the universe is prideful, *and slightly ridiculous!* There are few of us who have not tried to do it on our own at one time or another. But most often, when we rely on ourselves, we ultimately fail.

> *God opposes the proud but shows favor to the humble.*
> 1 Peter 5:5

Pride can grow in the soil of bitterness. A majority of the pride I deal with comes from a place of brokenness. It comes from things in my past that were "unfair." From a deep need inside me to be heard and not disregarded; a longing to be noticed and not passed over.

I have since learned who I am in Christ and have found my voice. But I can easily and unknowingly go too far. I can so desperately want to be heard, chosen or accepted that envy and resentment rear their ugly head. And at the heart of envy and resentment, is pride.

> *"Pride is spiritual cancer: it eats up the very possibility of love, or contentment, or even common sense."*[75]
> –C.S. Lewis, *Mere Christianity*

Kudos to American gospel and contemporary Christian recording artist, Mandisa, who skipped the Grammys in 2014 in order to keep her pride in check. What vulnerability she displayed. I admire those who know their weaknesses and limitations. What a great example for the rest of us.

> *"I have been struggling with being in the world, not of it lately. I have fallen prey to the alluring pull of flesh, pride, and selfish desires quite a bit recently."*[76]
> –Mandisa

Below is an excerpt from a 2014 interview with Billy Hallowell from *The Blaze*.

She said that putting herself in an environment that celebrates some of the elements she's trying to avoid was "risky," so she decided to stay home, as she is trying to renew her mind to become "the Heavenly Father-centered, completely satisfied with Jesus, and Holy Spirit-led woman" she once was.[77]

Christians often do not recognize the seriousness of the sin of pride. Many types of sins can be destructive, but pride is putting yourself above God. Nothing could be more offensive to Him. In order to have a close relationship with God, we must lift *Him* up. Acknowledging our position compared to Him leads to spiritual maturity.

It is so important that we, as Christians, do not stick our heads in the sand about pride. We need to face this adversary head on. We need to recognize the enemy if we are to defeat it.

Fighting pride is a continuous battle for all of us. We must be vigilant, never letting our guard down when it comes to pride. And, we need to teach our kids to be vigilant too.

Overcoming pride should be a daily prayer for us all.

Whoever wants to become great among you must be your servant, and whoever wants to be first must be your slave—just as the Son of Man did not come to be served, but to serve, and to give his life as a ransom for many.
Matthew 20:26-28

We must put down our pride. We must put it down daily.

"If anyone would like to acquire humility, I can, I think, tell him the first step. The first step is to realize that one is proud…If you think you are not conceited, it means you are very conceited indeed."[78]
–C.S. Lewis, *Mere Christianity*

If we do not stress the power of pride to our children, it is not likely that humility will grow in them. The world will teach them to be proud, not humble. Humility is essential to following Christ.

But God chose the foolish things of the world to shame the wise; God chose the weak things of the world to shame the strong. God chose the lowly things of this world and the despised things—and the things that are not— to nullify the things that are, so that no one may boast before him.
1 Corinthians 1:27-29

The Ride Home

It was the morning of the first day of school a couple years ago, and I was driving home from Starbucks. I ended up behind a school bus. My girls had already been gone for a couple of hours and my mind was occupied with my to-do list for the day.

I ended up behind the elementary school bus. My neighborhood has a long street that runs through the middle of it where the bus stops many times. The bus pulled up to the first stop where a group of parents were gathered with their little kids in dresses and new clothes and shiny backpacks. They were taking pictures as the kids looked back and waved before they stepped into the big bus.

A rush of memories flooded my mind and I started to sob.

My sweet little Jessica in her little green dress and pigtails on the first day of kindergarten and Emily's precious freckled face, or 'sprinkles' as we used to call them, and her strawberry shortcake backpack flashed before me. I missed those little girls. My heart ached for them. It seemed like such a long time ago.

As the red lights ceased to flash and the bus pulled away, I tried to collect myself. I was being silly. *Jeesh—get it together, Kim!* I told myself. I dried up and continued behind the bus. Fifteen seconds later we stopped again, and the whole scene repeated itself and I sobbed again. And fifteen seconds after that, and fifteen seconds after that. Each time I watched this beautiful milestone play out with moms and dads taking pictures and cheering on their little ones, I sobbed.

When I got home that day, I thought about my kids and how wonderful they were. I thanked God for the blessing of my family. I honestly didn't know how they turned out so great with me as their mom. I began to weep again. I knew they were wonderful and loved the Lord *in spite* of me, not *because* of me.

Friends and family members might say, "You've been a great mom, look at how wonderful your kids are, you did a great job." Although I appreciate their intentions and love, they are wrong. It's all because of God...*all of it!*

While pride is the root of every sin, humility is at the heart of every fruit of the spirit.

The opposite of pride is humility. And while pride is the root of every sin, humility is at the heart of every fruit of the spirit. Everything we do in our life will come out of one or the other. Not only must we actively fight against our prideful nature, we must also be intentional about exuding humility.

Our eyes need to stay on the prize. And the road to getting there is paved with humility.

Self-esteem and Our Kids

A few years ago, my daughter went on a junior high retreat. When she got back, I asked her what they talked about in their large group sessions. The only thing she could remember was self-esteem.

Self-esteem has been a hot topic since I was a teenager in the 80s. Anywhere there is a gathering of kids or youth, this seems to be a popular topic. Self-esteem is focusing inward, while God teaches us to focus outward and upward.

Self-esteem is focusing inward, while God teaches us to focus outward and upward.

Do nothing out of selfish ambition or vain conceit. Rather, in humility value others above yourselves, not looking to your own interests but each of you to the interests of the others.
Philippians 2:3-4

"Self-confidence, popularly conceived is not a virtue. It is a vice. It has at its root pride."[79]
–Paul Gould

I have always been a people pleaser. Humility is a natural thing for me almost more than pride is...*almost.*

Am I always humble? Absolutely not. I will always struggle with pride, with wanting what *I* want, and being selfish. I am human.

However, I had many challenges in childhood that caused me to think less of myself, or have "low self-esteem." Maybe this was a gift from God not a curse. Maybe I am capable of more humility now because I started out with such a low image of myself. If that is the case, then thank you God for low self-esteem!

Maybe because of my humble beginnings, I have been open to seeing how enormous God is. I didn't have to "get over myself" quite as much when elevating God in my life. I was never as much about myself to begin with. God showed me my great worth in Him and because of Him.

God has not been building me up through the years, He has been revealing more of Himself to me. I no longer care how small I may be. He is great and mighty and that gives my soul peace and freedom. Yes, I still believe that I am wretched, but I have been redeemed by an almighty God.

Let's teach our kids to highly esteem God, not themselves. That is what God asks of all of us. He asks us to be a servant to all. Just as Christ was.

In your relationships with one another, have the same mindset as Christ
Jesus: Who, being in very nature God, did not consider equality with
God something to be used to his own advantage; rather, he made himself
nothing by taking the very nature of a servant, being made in human
likeness. And being found in appearance as a man, He humbled Himself
by becoming obedient to death—even death on a cross!
Philippians 2:5-8

"Those on the self-confidence bandwagon are placing their identity in the
wrong thing! We ought not to be so confident in the self."[80]
–Paul Gould

Some teach their kids to love themselves, while God's Word teaches the exact opposite.

Anyone who loves their life will lose it, while anyone who hates their life in
this world will keep it for eternal life.
John 12:25

Teaching our kids to love themselves contradicts the Word of God. And it leads to pride.

What if instead of teaching kids that they should think highly of themselves, we taught them about the greatness of our God? What if instead of focusing on praising our kids, we focused on glorifying God who is high and lifted up? What if we focused not on what is temporal and will pass away, but on the surpassing worth of knowing Jesus Christ?

All the things I once thought were so important are gone from my life.
Compared to the high privilege of knowing Christ Jesus as my Master,
firsthand, everything I once thought I had going for me is insignificant—
dog dung. I've dumped it all in the trash so that I could embrace Christ
and be embraced by Him.
Philippians 3:8-9 (MSG)

If we taught our kids mainly about God's worth and the joy of knowing Him instead of loving themselves, the emotional health of future generations would greatly improve.

So, I am not going to teach my kids to love themselves, or worry about their "self-esteem." I am not going to go over the top with praise, or continuously feed their egos. I am going to teach them the surpassing worth of knowing Jesus Christ. Because of *Him,* they have great worth as God's beloved children.

Our kids' worth should come from being sons and daughters of the King. Their worth should come from knowing that God loves them so much that He sent His Son to die for each one of them. Their confidence should come from their identity in Christ.

A Selfish Core

My husband recently went to lunch with someone he used to work with. Let's call him Josh. He was having a hard time in his marriage and expressed that he was considering leaving her. I know his wife, and she has been dealing with extreme depression and health problems.

I had met Josh at a work party, and he seemed like a good guy. The more my husband got to know him, the more he realized that Josh had a selfish core he needed to deal with.

Good people can have a selfish core. They can be giving, kind and thoughtful to those around them. However, the core of who we are will come out in marriage if nowhere else. We hope that our spouses bring out the best in us, but marriage often brings out the worst. It forces all of our skeletons and ugliness to come to the surface. And we must face who we really are, not who we have pretended to be.

In the few years that Josh had been married, it had been a roller coaster ride of ups and downs, of highs and lows. The highs were wonderful, and the lows were dark.

Josh grew up being the youngest of three boys. They were all very much mama's boys. And his mom was very focused on their self-esteem.

His mother had a horrific experience with the church in her childhood. There was a lot of shaming, fear, and she always felt on the edge of losing her salvation. I am convinced that she has PTSD because of it. It is really heartbreaking knowing that churches can do so much damage.

Because of what was done to her, and her lifelong battle with shame and self-esteem, she wanted the opposite for her children. She was determined to raise kids who had a healthy self-esteem, and not the shame that she had always felt.

She hardly ever said *no* to the boys when they were growing up. Even when they became adults she still had a hard time even disagreeing with them. She didn't want to damage their self-esteem.

Where Josh's mom had a broken core, her boys developed a selfish core. And all things flow from our core.

Josh had expectations in his marriage that his wife often wasn't meeting. He didn't understand why. He was used to getting everything he wanted. My husband's mentoring relationship with him encouraged him to take a hard look at himself.

We need to be careful when we focus on our kid's self-esteem. It can, unintentionally, create a selfish core in them. If we focus on the goodness of God and their value in *Him,* our kids' core might be very different. They might be more like Jesus.

The strongest defining characteristic of Jesus after love, was humility. No one has ever been higher or more worthy of praise that walked this earth than Jesus Christ. And no one has ever been more humble.

If you want your kids to have faith in Christ, there is nothing that can make *Him* more attractive than a display of love and humility in *you.*

Chapter 8

Three Elements of a Contagious Faith: Third, Surrender

"The goal is to transition our children from total dependence on us to total dependence on Him. Our job is to teach them how to follow their true Father, their true Master. Then we let go because we have returned them to their rightful Owner."[81]
—Francis Chan, *You and Me, Forever*

I love stories. And I'm sure by now, you have picked up on the fact that I love movies. God uses them to teach me. Life lessons come alive through stories in movies. Seeing ourselves in the characters fosters understanding.

Novelist Pat Conroy beautifully illustrates the significance of stories to writers.

Stories are the vessels I use to interpret the world to myself... The most powerful words in English are "Tell me a story," words that are intimately related to the complexity of history, the origins of language, the continuity of the species, the taproot of our humanity, our singularity, and art itself.[82]

One of the greatest movies of all time is *Evan Almighty*. Despite the fact that Hollywood produced this film, it has some profoundly spiritual dialogue. And it is a wonderful family movie.

My favorite scene is when Evan first encounters God face to face. God, played by Morgan Freeman, wants him to build an ark. Evan is less than thrilled.

Evan: So, you're really him, aren't you?

God: Do you want more proof? I haven't done the pillar of salt thing in a while.

Evan: That's all right, I believe you. I just don't understand why you chose me.

God: You want to change the world son...So do I.

Evan: Why an ark? That's like flood territory. You wouldn't do that again. You wouldn't do that. Would you do that?

God: Let's just say, whatever I do, I do because I love you.

Evan: Well, then you have to understand that this whole building an ark thing is really not part of my plans here. I need to settle into my house. I need to make a good impression at work (is interrupted by God laughing) What?

God: (still laughing hysterically) Your plans. (more laughing)

I wonder if God gets a good chuckle out of our "plans."

I spent the first fifteen years of my adult life trying to be independent. Trying to live out "my plan." I was terrible at it. And, I was in bondage; the bondage of pleasing other people; the bondage of trying to be successful at things I was not created for; and, the bondage of proving my worth to myself and the world.

I wish I had known that *God* is the only One I needed to please. I wish I'd known that *God's* plan is the only one I needed to follow.

After much soul searching and prayer, I finally got it. God made me for a specific purpose, and He would lead me to it. Therefore, I didn't have to prove my worth to anybody. I only needed to keep my eyes on *Him*.

His purposes are higher than our plans.

We need to get out of the way and let God lead.

The third element of a contagious faith is *surrender*. Surrendering to God's authority leads to freedom. It's the only way.

It is for freedom that Christ has set us free. Stand firm, then, and do not let yourselves be burdened again by a yoke of slavery.
Galatians 5:1

We can experience true and complete freedom when we surrender our will to God. All areas of our life must be under the Lordship of Christ. If we truly love him above all things, we will use all areas of our lives to bring *Him* glory.

My husband, Jamie, is a wonderful man. And he is a wonderful father. I am truly blessed. However, as the breadwinner, he gets really stressed out about money. This area of his life can really eat him up. He has a hard time surrendering the family finances to God.

He becomes angry and discontent when he allows money to stress him out. However, the times when he has given it to God, months later he'll look back and realize how free and peaceful he has felt. God is faithful.

I, on the other hand, have a hard time surrendering my kids to God. I hold on tightly to the role I have of "mom."

Recently, there has been tension in our house between my oldest daughter, Emily, who just turned seventeen, and me. She and I have always butted heads. Maybe we're too much alike?

She is the kid who always pushes the boundaries, and bends the rules. She is my "strong-willed" child. Now, she is almost an adult and I need to turn her over to her Heavenly Father more and more. I need to trust that God has Emily in the palm of His hand.

Our kids belong to God, *He* is their Master and most perfect Father.

Our kids must see that God is the master of our lives, *ours and theirs*. If we resist allowing God Lordship over our life, our kids will likely resist Him, too. We must model surrender, which is paramount to the Christian faith.

We teach our kids to become independent from us. We teach them to tie their shoes, use the potty, do their homework, and clean their rooms. Basically, our job in the early years of parenting is to teach our kids how to take care of themselves and thrive in our society.

However, as our kids approach ten to twelve years of age, we need to be transitioning from mostly *parenting* to mostly *discipling*. Parenting—teaching our kids to take care of themselves in order to be a functioning member of society—should *decrease* as kids go through adolescence. At the same time, an emphasis on discipling and teaching kids to depend on God should *increase*.

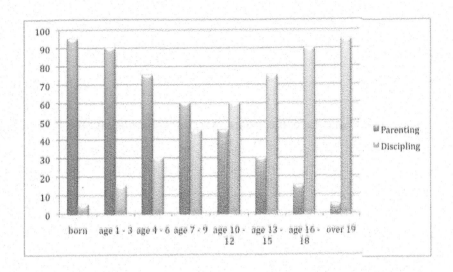

God calls us to make disciples, which starts in our homes, with our children.

Therefore go and make disciples of all nations, baptizing them in the name of the Father and of the Son and of the Holy Spirit.
Matthew 28:19

A disciple of Christ is someone who is surrendered to God. We will talk more about what it means to be a disciple in Chapter 9.

Age Appropriate

The other day I was cleaning off my bookshelf in my office. I had piles of homeschool materials collecting dust. I homeschooled my girls many years ago because Jessica was falling behind, and I wanted to catch her up.

As I was sorting out the materials for each school year, a thought hit me. Wow! Emily and Jessica have come so far. The material they are learning in school now as a sophomore and senior is way over my head. Emily has come a long way from fifth grade math to AP Calculus, and from general science to chemistry and physics.

We read Bible stories to our kids, take them to church, and teach them about God. However, when kids reach a certain point in their maturity, it is the time to address deeper aspects of the faith. Most often, however, we keep feeding our kids, who are not kids, but young men and women, a childish faith.

Just as we do in school, our teaching of the faith must evolve, as our kids get older. It would be silly to teach them the same things in third grade as we teach in tenth grade. As they get older, we must treat them like the young men and women they have become.

Teaching our kids to depend on God as they grow and mature is crucial. If they never learn how to truly surrender their life to Jesus, then their faith is not likely to last.

Then Jesus said to his disciples, "Whoever wants to be my disciple must deny themselves and take up their cross and follow me."
Matthew 16:24

As much as dependence on us should eventually be broken as our kids get older, complete independence should *not* be the goal. If parents are followers of Christ and are emphasizing independence as the goal for their children, then they are missing the mark.

Should our kids become independent from us, their parents? *Yes.* But, should our kids be taught to live completely independent lives and totally rely on themselves? *No.* Living a life completely reliant on oneself is exhausting, not to mention futile.

"God built dependency into all of us. We all need God and we need each other…God intended us to be incomplete in and of ourselves. Dependency is built by God into the very fabric of the universe."[83]
–Dr. Henry Cloud and Dr. John Townsend,
Twelve "Christian" Beliefs That Can Drive You Crazy

The goal in raising our kids is to move them from dependence on *us* to dependence on *God*; or, from being under our authority to being under the authority of God the Father.

Author and speaker Francis Chan said it best in a podcast when he said that the goal of Christian parenting is to raise our kids to be *independently dependent*.

What does it look like for parents to surrender completely to Christ?

- *spending time with God every day*
- *putting our spouse's needs above our own*
- *going where God calls us to go*
- *spending time serving others*
- *using our resources for God's glory*

What does it look like for our kids to surrender to Christ?

- *spending time with God every day*
- *submitting to His will regarding relationships*
- *spending time serving others*
- *following God's calling for their life*

Depending on God is not something we should assume our kids will do when they are adults. Parents need to model and encourage this dependence throughout their childhood and adolescence.

> *"The greatest gift you can give your children is to let them see you struggle and wrestle with how to live a lifetime of trust in God."*[84]
> –Dr. Kara Powell and Dr. Chap Clark, *Sticky Faith*

If our kids grasp the idea of reliance on God as teenagers, there is a far greater chance they will rely on God as adults. And a far greater chance they will stay in the faith.

Therefore, my dear brothers and sisters, stand firm. Let nothing move you.
Always give yourselves fully to the work of the Lord, because you know that
your labor in the Lord is not in vain.
1 Corinthians 15:55-57

The Magic Wallet

When my youngest daughter was little she used to talk about having a "magic wallet." Whenever we couldn't afford something, she would make up stories about a magic wallet, and we would giggle. We talked about how great it would be if we had a magic wallet when we wanted something we couldn't have.

Who wouldn't want to have a magic wallet, or for that matter, a magic wand? As parents, we would like to be able to assure our children that nothing bad will ever happen to them. Because if it does, we can just wave our magic wand and everything will be all right.

If it were totally up to parents, we would always be with our kids to protect them. We want to believe that we can protect them from anything and everything.

Unfortunately, that isn't reality. Tragedies and natural disasters happen every day. We can't stop them. And, tragedies happen to children.

Fires, earthquakes, tornadoes, and tsunamis can happen and no one can predict when or where with certainty. This is the world we live in. The reality is that we cannot keep our kids safe from everything that could happen in this life. It's not possible.

The older we get, the more aware of this we are.

Approximately three hundred thousand people died in the earthquake in Haiti in 2010. According to Rebecca Chandler, former child protection expert with the International Rescue Committee, "tens of thousands of Haitian children are homeless, traumatized, disoriented, and distressed, and those who have been separated from family members are especially vulnerable."[85]

In 2015, the earthquake near Kathmandu, Nepal, killed more than forty-eight hundred people and another ninety-two hundred plus were injured. The earthquake affected eight million people across Nepal. And as the one-year anniversary passed, one million children were still in desperate need of help.[86]

The movie, *The Impossible*, recounts the heartbreaking true story of the Bennett family who were vacationing for the Christmas holiday in Thailand when the devastating tsunami of 2004 hit. This story of courage and survival against insurmountable odds is breathtaking.

The movie tells the heart-wrenching story of this family's desperate search to find each other in the carnage. How helpless they must have felt. While they were eventually reunited, thousands of other families, who were looking for missing loved ones, were not.

Reports of the devastation of the 2004 tsunami from *National Geographic* magazine painted a horrifying picture.

> By the end of the day more than one hundred fifty thousand people were dead or missing and millions more were homeless in eleven countries…As many as a third of the people who died in the tsunami were children; many of them would not have been strong enough to resist the force of the water.[87]

What if something happened to my kids in a natural disaster like this? What if I couldn't get to them? Most parents can probably relate to this fear. Although we live in the most privileged society on the planet, the uncertainty of life is universal. Regardless of ethnicity, geographic location, economic status, or religion, uncertainty is the only certainty there is.

Uncertainty is the only certainty there is in this life.

We could stick our head in the sand and pretend that nothing could ever happen to our children. *Ignorance is bliss,* they say. Or, we can accept reality and prepare our kids for whatever might come their way.

In addition to natural disasters, evils such as war, terrorist attacks, school shootings, abductions, and violence exist in this world. Kids are as vulnerable as anyone—probably more so.

It was a Wednesday afternoon on December 2, 2015, and the smell of fresh laundry filled my bedroom. I was watching *Dr. Oz* as the cat purred shamelessly in the warmth of the clothes. Thoughts of things I needed to do before the kids got home from school raced through my head. *Empty the dishwasher, pick up food for dinner, finish blog post, take out the trash.* Then a reporter interrupted. Breaking News cut into the station just as the show was ending.

"Uh, oh, " I thought. The live video appeared.

An all too familiar scene played out before me on the television. A public place filled with cop cars and police officers in tactical gear; people lined up coming out of buildings with their hands in the air; paramedics and people on stretchers filled the streets.

It was the shooting in San Bernardino, California. Another tragedy. I couldn't imagine the grief and sorrow the families must have gone through. Not to mention the fear the community must have faced in the aftermath.

I also remember Columbine so many years ago. It was April 20th, 1999. Twelve students and one teacher were killed after Eric Harris and Dylan Klebold went on a violent rampage.[88] It was this nation's first big school shooting where students were killed, at least in recent history.

Gone were the days of feeling like our kids were safe when we sent them to school. Gone were the days of feeling safe going to work, to the mall, to a movie or to a concert. Gone were the days when we could drop off our kids at college and know they would be safe.

Gone are the "wonder years" in this country. Violence has come to our cities and towns.

I have tried to imagine what I would be feeling if a mass shooting happened in my town. How would I process it? How would I help my kids process it?

How would I be feeling if the Wal-mart five minutes from my house was on the news because a shooter was gunning down people there; or, an office building along US-31; or, my church just down 146th Street; or, the Regal 17 movie theater where I recently saw *Jurassic World.*

Tragedy can happen anywhere.

A couple of summers ago it seemed as though about every week or two we would hear about another shooting. One week it was a shooting in Texas. I can still see the face of the gunman with wild hair and that crazed look in his eyes I saw on the news.

Maybe, we as a country were ignorant. Little did we know how drastically our country, and the world, would change in the decades to come.

It's hard to believe it has been five years since the attack on Sandy Hook Elementary School in Newtown, Connecticut, where twenty kids and six adults were killed the morning of December 14, 2012. It was the second deadliest shooting in U.S. History after the massacre at Virginia Tech, where thirty-two students were killed.[89] The thought of it still makes me sick.

How could someone hurt little children? They were so young—practically babies.

To be honest, I didn't know how to feel about another tragedy. I felt torn between being filled with compassion and sympathy and feeling frustrated and angry. I was worn out with tragedy. The whole country was.

And then there is terrorism. The violence in Paris at the Bataclan in November of 2015, and the many attacks since, stand as sobering reminders that it is not just the United States that is under attack, it is the whole world.

A friend of mine's daughter, Carly, was right in the middle of the attacks in Nice, France on July 14, 2016. According to a BBC News article, "dozens of people were killed, including children, when a lorry (a motor truck, an especially large one) ploughed into a large crowd watching a fireworks display in Nice to mark the Bastille Day holiday."[90]

Thankfully, Carly was not hurt and quickly got a flight home the next morning before the airport was closed. I remember how relieved my friend felt when her daughter's plane landed on U.S. soil. I rejoiced with her and thanked God for protecting this precious child.

In 1993, the World Trade Center in New York City was bombed. Six people were killed and thousands were injured.[91] A couple years later in 1995, the Oklahoma City bombing killed 168 people, nineteen of which were young children in the building's day care center.[92]

And then there was 9/11. The most massive attack on U.S. soil. We all know where we were and what we were doing that fateful day. It was seared into our brains. Almost three thousand lives were lost on that tragic day, eight of them were children.[93] How many more children lost their moms and dads that day?

What do we do with all of this? Do we have a magic wand that can keep our kids safe from everything? Obviously not. So, how do we prepare our children for the harshness of this world?

We may not have a magic wand or a magic wallet, but we have been given everything we need.

> *His divine power has given us everything we need for a godly life through*
> *our knowledge of Him who called us by His own glory and goodness.*
> 2 Peter 1:3

The best way we can prepare our children for the hard realities of this world is by passing on a strong, passionate faith in Jesus Christ.

The Game-Changer

I was watching a movie one night when a scene from the Holocaust came up. The Nazis were forcing the Jews onto trains that would take them to the death camps. In the mud and rain, a young boy was violently separated from his parents. As the chasm between them grew, the boy screamed, and his mom and dad sobbed in desperation as they were restrained.

Scenes like this from movies are heartbreaking. What a dark time that was.

As a parent, you can't help but picture yourself in these poor parents' shoes. The strength of the soldiers overpowered them. What could they possibly have done as their child was being dragged away? They physically could not save him. Talk about a sobering reality.

Author and Holocaust survivor, Corrie ten Boom, endured the hardship and horror of the death camps of World War II. The faith this woman had is mind blowing. She was proof that God can shine His light into the darkest places.

"No pit is so deep that He is not deeper still."
–Corrie ten Boom

What if the boy from the movie knew what Corrie ten Boom knew? What if he knew without a shadow of a doubt that God loved him and that God is good? And, what if this young boy knew God would be with him even if his parents weren't. His frame of mind could be very different. He might have *hope.*

The Lord delights in those who fear Him, who put their hope in His
unfailing love.
Psalm 147:11

To hope is to look forward with desire and confidence; to feel that something desired may happen; to believe and trust. If we know God's promises of enduring love and constant presence, we have hope.

The God of comfort and peace is our hope in the midst of desperation. It is not enough to teach our kids to believe, we must teach them to have hope.

Hope is not only something we have, it is something we do. Hope is what gets us outside of ourselves and beyond the present moment. Hope tells us that we will be okay in the future, even if we aren't okay now. Hope looks beyond the present circumstances to a glorious future.

**Hope gets us outside of ourselves and beyond
the present moment.**

I have often wondered how the parents of the children who were killed in the Sandyhook Elementary School massacre could survive. How do parents survive the death of a child? Being a parent, I can't imagine it.

Not only am I a movie buff, but I find movies helpful in my understanding of God. He certainly can use all things for good. If you are like me, you need to be *shown* to understand.

The movie *Manchester by the Sea,* illustrates what life looks like without God. *(warning: spoiler alert!)* A man accidentally caused a fire that resulted in the death of his children. He never recovered from it. He never moved past it. Joy was no longer possible and tragedy defined him. He was a man without hope.

Hope in Christ is our greatest reward. It offers us freedom, brings about peace, and promises us a future that is far better than what we have now. Hope is born from knowing God and trusting in His promises. The more we know Him, the more hope we have.

Though an army besiege me, my heart will not fear.
Psalm 27:3

The end point of our faith is an eternity with God in heaven. It is one of God's greatest promises to us.

No matter how difficult, impossible, or hopeless things might seem, we are promised joy, happiness, and euphoria in Heaven with God. In paradise, where there are no more tears, no more trials, and no more suffering, we will dwell with God forever. Knowing this is our future can sustain us through tough times.

Praise be to the God and Father of our Lord Jesus Christ! In His great mercy He has given us new birth into a living hope through the resurrection of Jesus Christ from the dead, and into an inheritance that can never perish, spoil or fade.
1 Peter 1:3-4

What if the boy from the movie had hope? How would a young person's experience of tragedy or its aftermath be different if they had the Holy Spirit living inside of them? Would his state of mind be different? Is it possible when facing trauma, for our children to benefit from a personal faith in Christ?

If kids have a deep faith and hope in Christ they might not be wounded or permanently scarred from traumatic experiences. Instead of falling into terror or depression, remaining afraid and jaded, or being defined by tragedy, they can move through trials and be okay on the other side. They will be able to process the experience without it changing them or causing their heart to harden.

Still, having hope and knowing God's truths does not guarantee there will be no pain and suffering. The boy from the movie would still be forced onto the train apart from his parents and be sent to a death camp. He would still endure trauma, *major* trauma. It would be painful. He would be cold, lonely, starving, and scared. His circumstances may not change, he still could be killed, but, he wouldn't be alone. If he knew that, even to a small degree, it could be a game-changer. Just as it was for Corrie ten Boom.

Middle School or Middle Earth?

The movie, *Lord of the Rings,* takes place in a dark, dangerous, and foreboding place called Middle Earth. It's filled with all kinds of grotesque creatures.

Middle school is like Middle Earth.

When Jessica, my youngest daughter, was in middle school, the teacher asked the kids in gym class to find a partner and go sit against the wall. Everyone paired up except Jessica. She couldn't find a partner, so she was left standing humiliated in front of her classmates. With twenty pairs of eyes on her, embarrassment and rejection filled her body and soul. "Hold it together, don't cry, don't cry," she told herself.

As I pictured Jessica standing in front of everybody, mortified, I felt a knife puncture my heart and twist until it came out the other side. I had to talk myself out of going to the school and giving the gym teacher a piece of my mind. There is nothing more painful for a parent than to hear a story like that. *Ugh!*

It's so hard to coach a kid on what to do in this kind of situation. There are no answers that are good enough. She was humiliated. And it hurt her deeply to be left standing there all alone.

However, if she is being discipled and growing in her faith, she is less likely to internalize the situation. She may be less likely to turn this into a defining moment in her life. And she may be less likely to let the situation affect her sense of identity.

If she has hope, it might not be so damaging. In the locker room after class she could remind herself of verses that tell her how valuable she is, and how much God loves her, and the arrows of pain and rejection might not penetrate quite so deep.

Our kids don't have to go through scary things alone. It is our job to prepare them for the valleys of life they will inevitably face. We can't always be with them, but God can. The sooner kids learn that our God is the God of all compassion and comfort, and that He is always with them, the less damaging hard times will be.

What hope do we have? What does God promise us?

When you pass through the waters, I will be with you; and when you pass through the rivers, they will not sweep over you. When you walk through the fire, you will not be burned; the flames will not set you ablaze.
Isaiah 43:2

We need to teach our kids to go to God when they walk through the valleys; when pain, despair, or disappointments flood their lives. If they develop this practice early on, when trials hit, they will know where to turn. And, they might have hope.

Am I Enough?

At one time or another, most kids wonder if they are enough. They may fear they don't have what it takes to be loved, to succeed, or find their way. I know I did in my youth. Being a kid today is tough. The many pressures they face can weigh heavily on them. They may wonder *am I smart enough? Are my parents proud of me? Am I special?*

Several years ago, the theme of the youth ministry at my church was "He is Enough." *Christ* is all we need. What a simple concept, yet so profound. Understanding this concept can give life, freedom, and hope to a lost world.

And my God will meet all your needs according to the riches
of his glory in Christ Jesus.
Philippians 4:19

The Christian faith often comes down to such simple principles. God doesn't expect us to bring much to the table. All we need is faith and a willing heart. It is so important that we teach our kids that *He* is enough. And with Him, we are too.

How would our lives be different if we lived as if we believed this virtue? Would we worry and fret as we do now? Oh, the freedom that could be ours and our children's if we believed that God is enough.

My grace is sufficient for you.
2 Corinthians 12:9

A couple years ago, my family and I went to a graduation open house. The house was bustling with high schoolers and family and friends. My cousin, the graduate's mom, joked that it was like a "happy funeral" because all of their sets of friends and family who didn't know each other were there. We had a good laugh.

When we got home, my husband and I talked about another open house we had coming up. Most of our friends' kids were not graduating yet, so we only had a couple to go to. This one was for the son of a good friend of ours. I had been looking forward to it for months. This friend had been stressed about it so I had been praying for her.

"When is the other open house?" my husband inquired.

I thought it was coming up, but I couldn't find it on the calendar. So I looked at the invitation on the fridge. It read June 1st. *I had missed it!* My heart fell out of my chest.

How could I have missed it?! What kind of friend am I? How could I have let this happen?! Everybody was probably there except us—*the losers who couldn't read a calendar!* After I sufficiently berated myself, I started to wonder, as I often do, if I am enough. I certainly didn't feel like it in that moment.

Regardless of our failures, mistakes, and misdeeds, we can be sure that we are loved and forgiven.

Insecurities cause us to feel like we don't have anything to offer. We might feel worthless or like a failure from time to time. Because we will fail. But God can use whatever we have. He needs very little from us to fulfill His work. And we are *never* a failure in His eyes.

He who began a good work in you will carry it on to completion until the day of Christ Jesus.
Philippians 1:6

In 2 Kings 4, a woman's husband had died and she was going to lose her children if she didn't pay off all of her debts. All she had was a single bottle of oil. The prophet Elisha told her to go to her neighbors and ask for empty jars, lots of empty jars. So she did what he told her to do, and they took the jars home and started to pour oil in them.

When all the jars were full, she said to her son, "bring me another one." But he replied, "There is not a jar left." Then the oil stopped flowing. She went and told the man of God, and he said, "Go, sell the oil and pay your debts. You and your sons can live on what is left."
2 Kings 4:6-7

God is always enough. There is no need He cannot fill.

We were made with God-shaped holes in us. Without Him, we are incomplete. It doesn't matter how much or how little we have, because *He* is enough.

Letting Go

Not only should we teach our kids to depend on God, but we also have to let them. Most parents would agree that it's one thing to put our lives in God's hands, but it is quite another to put our *kids'* lives in God's hands.

My family is very close. We have chosen not to live a super busy life so my girls are home most of the time. They like being home and being with us. So, when they are gone, there is a hole in our family. We feel the void.

A couple summers ago both my daughters had trips to go on. As I kissed my youngest daughter Jessica, goodbye, there was a pit in my stomach and I felt almost sick. She was going to a junior high retreat only two hours away. And I would see her in five short days.

I knew it was good for her to go. I knew she would be fine. And I knew that I couldn't keep my girls under my wings forever. But mama bear never feels quite right unless all her children are home under her roof.

A week and a half after she got home my other daughter, Emily, went on a mission trip with the church youth group. They went to Honduras for ten days...*ten days*! Not only was she gone for what seemed like an eternity, but she went to another country without us. Needless to say, it was a rough month.

Fear can be a powerful thing in the life of a parent. We must not forget that God is bigger than any fear we might have. That is why we must pray, and trust.

God is good. And God is able. Our kids are in much better hands when they are in God's hands.

If our kids are going to follow Christ, their lives might involve risk. They might travel to a foreign country, be in the company of prisoners, drug dealers, or dangerous people, or go to places that we may consider unsafe. We must let them serve Christ wherever He leads them.

Reggie Joiner writes in his book, *Beyond Your Capacity:* "The ultimate mission of the family is not to protect your children from all harm but to mobilize them for the mission of God...It is possible to hold on to our kids so tightly that we forget the ultimate goal of parenting is to let go."[94]

Chapter 9

Oh, to be Like You

Grace, what have you done?
Murdered for me on that cross
Accused in absence of wrong
My sin washed away in your blood
Too much to make sense of it all
I know that your love breaks my fall
The scandal of grace, you died in my place
So my soul will live,
—"Scandal of Grace," Hillsong United

When I was younger, I read *The Oath*, by Frank Peretti, author of *This Present Darkness*. It was about a predator stalking the people of a mining town in the mountains of the Pacific Northwest. The predator struck the people of the town with a black stain, which represented the darkness of sin. As time passed, the stain grew larger until, one by one, each person was consumed.

What a great visual representation of a fallen world in need of a savior. All of us have had a black stain of sin on us. This story vividly shows the need for the redemptive blood of Jesus, because without it, we can never be clean.

> *But thanks be to God! He gives us the victory through*
> *our Lord Jesus Christ.*
> 1 Corinthians 15:57

Can you imagine carrying a lifetime of sins and failures on your back? The weight would be crushing.

We are freely given a fresh start through the death and resurrection of Christ Jesus. Salvation is what saves us from the righteous judgement of God. This amazing gift gives us life when we deserve death.

When it comes to gifts from God, however, salvation is just the tip of the iceberg. Even greater is the gift of *reconciliation*.

The Greek word for reconciliation means "restoration to favor."[95]

> *"Reconciliation…is a divine provision by which God's holy displeasure*
> *against alienated sinners is appeased, His hostility against them removed,*
> *and a harmonious relationship between Him and them established.*
> *Reconciliation occurs because God was graciously willing to design a way to*
> *have all the sins of those who are His removed from them"*[96]
> —John MacArthur

If we accept Jesus as Lord, we are no longer going to hell, which is what we deserve as sinners. Let's celebrate that. However, being *reconciled* to God through the precious blood of the Lamb is pretty amazing too. We can't leave that piece out. We will miss everything if we do.

Reconciliation with God is the key to an abundant life. The greatest part of the human experience is knowing God and being in relationship with Him.

We couldn't know God or even be in His presence if He didn't make a way for us to be reconciled to Him.

The greatest part of the human experience is knowing God and being in relationship with Him.

All this is from God, who reconciled us to himself through Christ and gave us the ministry of reconciliation.
2 Corinthians 5:18

We all have sinned and fallen short of the glory of God (Romans 3:23). Because of our sinfulness, we had a broken relationship with God. We need the redemptive blood of Jesus to restore a right relationship with God. We must recognize and acknowledge this most precious gift.

Conversion

Paul wrote that if we are in Christ, we will be a new creation.

Therefore, if anyone is in Christ, the new creation has come: The old has gone, the new is here!
2 Corinthians 5:17

The process of reconciliation and conversion requires something from God and something from us. God has done His part. The question always is, *have we done ours?*

"In short, we need to get back to a focus on conversion…It is converted students who go on to love Jesus and serve the church."[97]
—Jon Nielson

Believing that Jesus is the Son of God does not equal conversion. Praying the sinner's prayer does not equal conversion. Believing in Jesus and accepting Him are first steps in giving our life over to God. However, it can't stop there. It is not enough that our kids believe.

You believe that there is one God. Good! Even the demons believe that.
James 2:19

There is a difference between believing and following and it starts with converting. *Conversion is the key.*

John Piper, author of *Desiring God,* makes a distinction between knowledge and true conversion.

Conversion then involves repentance (turning from sin and unbelief), and faith (trusting in God alone for salvation). They are really two sides of the same coin...This means that saving faith in Christ always involves a profound change of heart. It is not merely agreement with the truth of a doctrine.[98]

Conversion, which plays an important role in whether our kids continue in the faith or drift away, is a *process* of repentance and faith.

Repentance and Faith

According to Google Translate, the Greek word for repentance is *metanoeō*/μετανοέω and *metanoia*/μετάνοια, which indicates a change of mind, a change in the behavior and actions, and a change in the inner nature; intellectual, intentional, and moral.

Simply put, repentance means we must be *changed.*

If we say that we have been converted but have not turned from our sinful ways, than we are being deceived. There cannot be a conversion without a "turning" from something.

What sin do most kids need to turn from? Ask your kids what they think.

- *pride*
- *selfishness*
- *passing judgment*
- *rebellious attitude*
- *gossip*
- *laziness*

If you are brave, you can also ask your kids what sins they think you need to turn from. This would be a great display of humility, which is one of the elements of a contagious faith we talked about in Chapter 7.

Faith is the other side of the coin of conversion. Faith is trusting in God for our salvation and trusting in His Word. Having faith is how we build our foundation on Christ.

However, "Faith is the effect of new birth, not the cause of it."[99] Piper writes.

The Life Cycle of a Disciple

If someone would have asked me if I was a disciple twenty years ago, I would have said, no. Disciples were the guys that walked with Jesus in the New Testament, you know, Peter, James, John, etc. Obviously, my understanding of the word was very limited.

Very few Christians grasp the concept of what it means to be a disciple. How can we go out and make disciples of all nations if we don't understand what a disciple is?

According to Google, the word *disciple* means a follower of Christ. It also means a follower or student of a teacher, leader, or philosopher. Therefore, if we want to call ourselves disciples, then we must be a student of Jesus Christ and follow Him.

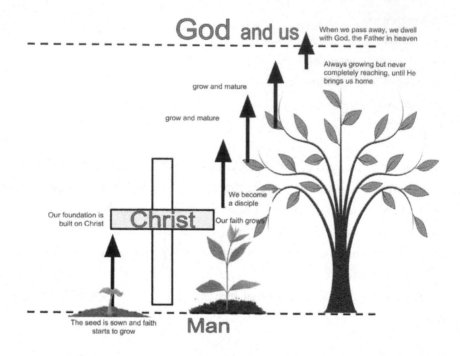

This illustration shows the life cycle of a disciple. What does the life of a disciple look like? First, the seed is sown in good soil in order for faith to grow.

Next, we build our foundation on Christ, and we begin to grow in Him. Finally, we grow and mature as a disciple as we move toward God, this lifelong process is called *sanctification*.

The Greek word for sanctification means "holiness." Therefore, to sanctify, in the Greek, means to "make holy."[100]

Are we seeking holiness in our character?

A disciple is always a work in progress. Disciples should always be growing and maturing as we are sanctified by the Holy Spirit.

They will be called oaks of righteousness, a planting of the LORD for the display of his splendor.
Isaiah 61:3

We must encourage our kids to build their foundation on Christ, become a disciple, and grow and mature spiritually. And we must teach them the goal in the character of a follower of Christ is holiness through sanctification.

Golden Triangle of Spiritual Transformation

Dallas Willard, in his book, *The Great Omission,* talks about the process of "putting on" the Lord Jesus Christ. "This process could be presented in a golden triangle of spiritual formation."[101]

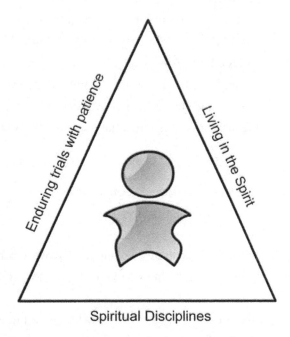

Spiritual Disciplines

Willard writes that for spiritual transformation to take place, we must endure trials with patience, live in the Spirit, and make spiritual disciplines a part of our daily lives.

Enduring Trials with Patience

One beautiful summer evening, some friends and I from church were out to dinner. Somehow, the state of the world and ISIS became the topic of conversation. I could hear the fear in their voices and see it in their eyes. "We aren't safe anymore!" my friend said. A couple of them continued to express how worried they were about it.

I tried to interject that we don't have to worry because, *He who is in you is greater than he who is in the world (1 John 4:4)*. But, they dismissed me and went back to fretting.

As they continued feeding on each other's fears, I wondered, *are they expressing these same worries in front of their kids?* These are the moments that speak loudly to our kids about our faith. What does our faith look like in times of extreme fear, strife, or uncertainty?

At some point we have to ask ourselves if we believe what God promises us in His Word. We can't have an "I do believe, but..." faith. There is no "but" about it. Either we believe Him or we don't.

We tend to worry and act as if we are caught off guard when trials or tragedy strikes. Whether it is the threat of terrorism, who is in the White House, or the flu going around, many Christians worry instead of putting their trust in God.

> *Do not be anxious about anything.*
> Philippians 4:6

Our kids will see the inconsistency in our faith if we worry excessively. Not only is worrying being disobedient to God, it can negatively impact the faith of our kids.

God warned us about the troubles of this world. He did not leave us to be surprised by calamity, blind-sided by disappointment, or unequipped for the hardships of this life. If we read God's Word, we know to expect trouble. The Bible is fraught with warnings of difficulty, trials, and danger.

> *In this world you will have trouble. But take heart! I have overcome the world.*
> John 16:33

The world is watching how we handle trials. And our kids are watching. Will we be patient and expectant? Will we trust God through the storms? Will we handle difficult situations like we have an almighty God on our side?

Through trials, we have the opportunity to show the world God's faithfulness.

"Don't tell God how big the storm is,
tell the storm how big your God is."[102]
—Joyce Burlingame, *Living with Death, Dying with Life*

Living in the Spirit

We have two choices. We can live by our flesh, or we can live by the Spirit. If we desire to be a disciple and grow spiritually, we must live by the Spirit. The Spirit and the flesh are contrary to each other. They cannot coexist.

Walk by the Spirit, and you will not gratify the desires of the flesh. For the
flesh desires what is contrary to the Spirit, and the Spirit what is contrary
to the flesh.
Galatians 5:16,17

In order to recognize what it is to walk in the Spirit, we must first recognize what it is *not*. Scripture makes clear in Galatians 5 the behaviors that indicate we are walking in the flesh.

- *sexual immorality*
- *impurity and debauchery*
- *idolatry*
- *hatred*
- *discord*

- *jealousy*
- *fits of rage*
- *selfish ambition*
- *dissensions*
- *envy*
- *drunkenness*

These behaviors indicate that we are walking in the flesh. And we need to repent.

If we walk in the Spirit, what kind of person will we be?

> *For this very reason, make every effort to add to your faith goodness; and to goodness, knowledge; and to knowledge, self-control; and to self-control, perseverance; and to perseverance, godliness; and to godliness, mutual affection; and to mutual affection, love.*
> 2 Peter 1:5-7

Walking in the Spirit can change our nature. Scripture says that we can participate in the *divine* nature.

> *Through these He has given us His very great and precious promises, so that through them you may participate in the divine nature.*
> 2 Peter 1:4

As our nature changes, the fruit of the spirit will naturally flow out from us as well.

- *Do we gossip about the neighbors?*
- *Do we judge our friends at church?*
- *Do we demand retribution when we have been wronged?*
- *Are we absorbed in our ambitions?*

Is it obvious to our kids that we are walking in the Spirit? Or, do they see us walking in the flesh?

Spiritual Disciplines

The third side of the triangle involves the practice of spiritual disciplines that transform us to reflect the image of Christ.

1. solitude
2. prayer
3. study
4. humility
5. service
6. worship
7. unity

Solitude

God and I have a good thing going. Our times together are amazing. There is nothing like someone as small and insignificant as me being in the presence of the almighty God. I can be totally vulnerable and still be totally loved and accepted. There is nothing to worry about, nothing to fear, nothing to make me feel bad or dirty, and no reason to feel like I don't belong. I can just enjoy His perfect peace.

Solitude is a spiritual discipline.

"Evangelicalism has a hearing problem. We often preach before we seek to understand a situation or before we sit in prayerful silence."[103]
–Adam S. McHugh, *Introverts in the Church*

A friend of mine recently attended a conference in which the theme was "Spacious Places." They were talking about spacious places not in terms of a *where*, but in terms of a *who*. In other words, God is our spacious place.

He brought me out into a spacious place;
He rescued me because He delighted in me.
Psalm 18:19

I have spent significant time in solitude in the last five or so years. I am very fortunate to be able to work from home, which allows me a flexible schedule and a quiet house. Some of my most profound inspirations or revelations happen when I have space; when I have quiet; and, when I spend time in solitude. This is when I hear God's voice.

The Lord is in His holy temple; let all the earth be silent before Him.
Habakkuk 2:20

Wisdom can be gained from solitude. If I were to write my own proverb, it would go something like this: "When we are listening, we learn. When we are silent, we hear. Silent observers gain much wisdom."

When we are listening, we learn.
When we are silent, we hear.

If one wants to gain wisdom, the best way to do it is to be quiet. Silence is a great teacher.

Jesus also spent time alone talking to God. He valued solitude. If we are to imitate Him, than this is a practice that we must adopt.

At daybreak, Jesus went out to a solitary place.
Luke 4:42

Prayer

The most powerful and spiritually transforming thing we can do is pray. Prayer adds power to our faith. We can't have a close relationship with God without it. And, just like any other relationship, it takes time.

> *"Don't pray when you feel like it. Have an appointment with the Lord and keep it. A man is powerful on his knees."*
> –Corrie ten Boom

I used to be mostly a casual prayer. Casual prayer throughout the day is a good thing. It usually means that you are walking in the Spirit. However, I started adding a time of prayer on my knees; a time of prayer that is more formal and focused. When I focus on His holiness and His greatness and am on my knees before Him, it changes me from the inside out.

We must teach our kids the power of prayer and that it is essential to the Christian faith. As a follower of Christ, prayer should be a regular part of their life.

> *Pray without ceasing.*
> 1 Thessalonians 5:17

Study of Scripture

Studying the Word of God is an important spiritual discipline. How else are we to know Him?

Someone once said to me, "I can't get myself to read the Bible. When I feel closest to God is when I am hiking or in nature, so maybe that is how I need to spend my time with God. I am just not a reader."

We all experience God in different ways. Some of us experience Him more through art or music or nature. My brother experiences the spirit of God when he is watching debates by famous apologists. All of these ways of experiencing God are equally valuable and the more of them we can appreciate, the richer our faith will be.

However, nothing can be a substitute for reading Scripture. Whether we like to read or not, it is critical that we immerse ourselves in His Word. Coupled with prayer, it is our lifeline.

> *Keep this Book of the Law always on your lips; meditate on it day and night, so that you may be careful to do everything written in it.*
> Joshua 1:8

Humility and Serving

As we talked about in Chapter 7, humility is foundational to our faith, and is a crucial element of a contagious faith. Humility and serving are also spiritual disciplines. Therefore, we must adopt a servant's heart.

The story in John 13 in which Jesus washed His disciple's feet must have been surreal.

> *Jesus answered, "Unless I wash you, you have no part with me."*
> John 13:8

I often contemplate how I would react if Jesus wanted to wash my feet? I can't even fathom the absurdity of it. He was the Son of God, after all. He was a King. How could I let *Him* wash *my* feet? How could anybody?

As crazy as it must have sounded to the disciples, Jesus had a purpose for doing it. Whether it was to teach us to be servants, or, if there was a higher purpose, His message was loud and clear.

> *Now that I, your Lord and Teacher, have washed your feet, you also should wash one another's feet. I have set you an example that you should do as I have done for you. Very truly I tell you, no servant is greater than his master, nor is a messenger greater than the one who sent him.*
> John 13:14-16

Worship

Everything that we do in our daily lives should be a form of worship to God. However, we need to set aside time to give Him praise. If we spend intentional, uninterrupted time worshiping Him, our love for Him will grow.

There is something almost magical about musical worship. While we send up praises to the heavens, God rains down love and healing on us. Through the act of worship, we are blessed. Everything was created to bring *Him* glory—especially music.

Unity

As a church body, we are told to love one another in unity. This was Jesus' prayer for all believers.

> *I have given them the glory that you gave me, that they may be one as*
> *we are one— I in them and you in me—so that they may be brought to*
> *complete unity. Then the world will know that you sent me and have loved*
> *them even as you have loved me.*
> John 17:22-23

We must strive for unity among the community of believers. Unity and love should be the goal of our churches.

Counting the Cost

I felt somewhat disillusioned about the faith growing up in my church. I was never taught the cost of discipleship. I was never taught that I was supposed to even *become* a disciple. In fact, I don't remember the word *disciple* being discussed at all.

One of the failings of the church is it doesn't teach that if we want to follow Jesus, we must become disciples. *And,* that there is a cost.

Jesus didn't pull any punches when He addressed the crowd following Him in Luke 14.

Large crowds were traveling with Jesus, and turning to them He said:
"If anyone comes to Me and does not hate father and mother, wife and
children, brothers and sisters—yes, even their own life—such a person
cannot be My disciple. And whoever does not carry their cross and follow
Me cannot be My disciple.
Luke 14:25-27

What must Jesus have been thinking when He turned around and saw crowds following Him? Based on His response, I would imagine Jesus knew many of these people did not know what they were getting into.

Jesus didn't want anyone following Him blindly. Right off the bat, He tells them they must hate their mother and father, brother and sister, and even their own life if they are going to follow Him.

It seems that Jesus was separating the wheat from the chaff. He was weeding them out. And then, He goes on to talk about the cost.

Suppose one of you wants to build a tower. Won't you first sit down and
estimate the cost to see if you have enough money to complete it? For if you
lay the foundation and are not able to finish it, everyone who sees it will
ridicule you, saying, "This person began to build and wasn't able to finish."

Or suppose a king is about to go to war against another king. Won't he first
sit down and consider whether he is able with ten thousand men to oppose
the one coming against him with twenty thousand? If he is not able, he
will send a delegation while the other is still a long way off and will ask for
terms of peace. In the same way, those of you who do not give up everything
you cannot be my disciples.
Luke 14:28-33

Following Jesus was not as easy as some of them thought. I wonder if people were stunned when they heard this. I wonder how many of them left.

From this Scripture, what is Jesus asking them to do if they wanted to follow Him?

- *turn your back on your family*
- *hate your own life*
- *carry your cross*
- *give up everything*

Jesus was not impressed with huge numbers of people. He wanted *disciples*.

We must teach our kids about the reality of following Jesus. And we must teach them to count the cost.

Part III

Discipleship Parenting

Chapter 10

Truth, Reality, and the American Dream

"The American Dream has become a death sentence of drudgery, consumerism, and fatalism: a garage sale where the best of the human spirit is bartered away for comfort, obedience and trinkets. It's unequivocally absurd."
–Zoltan Istvan, *The Transhumanist Wager*

In his 1931 book, *Epic of America*, historian, James Truslow Adams caused the phrase "American Dream" to become popular. At that time, America was suffering in the Great Depression, which according to History.com, was the deepest and most sustained economic downturn in the history of the Western, industrialized world.[104]

Jobs were scarce. Families were torn apart. Bread lines, soup kitchens, and unemployment were on the rise. The times brought the strongest of men to their knees.

As the country came out of the Great Depression, parents wanted to ensure that their kids would not want for anything. So they pointed their kids to the American Dream and nudged them on their way.

At a young age, my grandpa worked as a mail boy in a steel mill to support his brother and sister when his parents died. Times were tough. Through his hard work and sacrifice, his three kids grew up to be successful and prosperous. Since then, in my family, each generation has been "better off" than the one before.

As a society, we seem to exist mostly in extremes. American society is like a swinging pendulum. It picks up so much momentum as it swings, that it can't stop at a happy medium. We, as a society, have swung from one extreme to the other—from the Great Depression to the American Dream.

Wikipedia defines the American Dream as "a set of ideals in which freedom includes the opportunity for prosperity and success, and an upward social mobility for the families and children, achieved through hard work in a society with few barriers."[105]

I grew up in the suburbs thinking that life was all about the American Dream. Everything around me—the media, the community, the schools, my parents and even my church reinforced this ideal.

I knew the expected course of my life. I would get an education, get a job and climb the corporate ladder. I would make enough money to afford a nice house in the suburbs. And I would marry and have two or three kids, a dog, and a minivan. I would work for thirty to forty years in a career and retire comfortably at age sixty-five.

However, as I got older, I started to see the cost of the American Dream. We have become a society driven by power, greed, and selfish ambition.

Some of the unintended byproducts of the American Dream include:

- *working long hours*
- *acquiring debt*
- *failing in our marriages*
- *living beyond our means*
- *strained relationships*

And, most significantly, the American Dream is a distraction from what is *real*.

Back in the late 90s a movie called *The Matrix* was popular. Morpheus, the leader of a rebellion against the "Matrix" confronts Neo, the "chosen one," whose destiny is to defeat the machines that now control the human race.

Morpheus tells Neo at the beginning that what he sees and believes to be real around him, is in fact *not* real. And he is offered a choice. If he takes the blue pill, he will go back to life as he knew it blissfully unaware of the Matrix. If he takes the red pill, the reality of the Matrix would be revealed. He takes the red pill and his eyes are opened to the truth.

Truth can be painful, dirty, and dark. And sometimes to defend truth, we must go to war.

The American Dream doesn't seem to represent much truth or reality. Mainstream America is one of the most difficult mission fields in the world.

My thirteen year old daughter played recreational soccer years ago. Every spring and fall we spent our weekends on the soccer fields. In private, I did my share of grumbling. I have never enjoyed being a soccer mom. I don't do it well.

My husband and I went to every game we could and sat in the blazing hot sun or in the freezing cold rain to support her. As I outwardly cheered for her and the team, I sometimes prayed silently that they would lose, so we didn't have to go to the finals. *I know, I know...I am a terrible parent!*

I remember the spring she told me she didn't want to play soccer anymore. I was relieved, I'm not going to lie. But it led me to contemplate if I should let her. Is it acceptable for a thirteen-year-old girl to be home after school and in the evenings during the week? Or must she always have activities? Must she always be *busy*?

Teenagers being in two or three after-school activities is common. People look at you weird if your kids aren't in sports and/or busy all of the time.

The things we emphasize for our kids in America are academic excellence, sports, achievement, and strength. These are all things that many parents would say prepare their children for the future.

However, we must ask ourselves, *what kind of future are we preparing our kids for?* The American Dream? Or, God's will for their life?

Walt Mueller in his book, *Youth Culture 101* quotes Tom Sine who talks about Christians living in both worlds, and how it affects our kids.

> Author and cultural analyst Tom Sine says this: "To the extent that our secular culture's values captivate us, we are unavailable to advance God's Kingdom...We all seem to be trying to live the American Dream with a little Jesus overlay." If we fail to model and teach our kids about true faith, we'll only hurt our kids. And the cultural-generational gap will continue to grow.[106]

On the treadmill one morning I noticed something as I was watching the morning news show, *Good Morning America*. The thought hit me—*this isn't real.*

As I watched the polished hosts banter with one another and talk about shoes, wrinkle cream, and Kim Kardashian, my mind went numb. People were gathered around the fences outside of Rockefeller Center trying desperately to get a glimpse of Pitbull, John Legend, Miley Cyrus, or whoever was on that day.

Most of these morning shows focus on celebrities, fashion and beauty, and Hollywood drama. It's usually the who's who of Hollywood, flashing their pearly whites at the camera. And the successful, the beautiful, and the rich and powerful are deified. Hollywood and what we see on television are the epitome of the American Dream.

When we are mesmerized with the American Dream, we can't fully be used by God. Satan wants to keep us in a dream-like state to keep us distracted. The American Dream life generally correlates with our will, not God's will for our life.

When we are mesmerized with the American Dream, we can't fully be used by God.

You are all children of the light and children of the day. We do not belong
to the night or to the darkness. So then, let us not be like others, who are
asleep, but let us be awake and sober.
1 Thessalonians 5:5-6

The American Dream could be represented by the "Capital" in the movie *The Hunger Games*. In this futuristic world, the Capital is the place where the rich, privileged people lived. There, everything is sparkly, clean, and colorful. The citizens in the Capital are strange people. It was an obvious fantasy world. It wasn't *real*. What was real were the "districts" where food was scarce, oppression was real, and life in general was hard.

Fact Checking

Generations of young people are brought up with a distorted sense of reality. Morning news programs, talk shows, and network programming emphasize the importance of youth, beauty, and celebrity. We are told:

- *Outward beauty is of the highest value.*
- *Youth has more value than experience and wisdom.*
- *Celebrities are on a higher plane than the rest of us.*
- *The American Dream defines success.*

We must teach our kids to ask themselves constantly, is this real? Or is this the American Dream? The only way to answer those questions is to check it against the Word of God.

Therefore do not be foolish, but understand what the Lord's will is.
Ephesians 5:17

Fact Check: Is outward beauty important?

As a mother of two daughters, beauty is an issue I am constantly addressing. My girls' quest for physical perfection has lead to many teaching moments.

The messy entanglements of beauty and identity are pervasive in our culture. Too many wives, mothers, sisters, and daughters are slaves to beauty.

Although we were made beautiful and acceptable through the blood of the Lamb, somewhere along the way, we were deceived.

> *Charm is deceptive, and beauty is fleeting; but a woman who fears the Lord is to be praised.*
> Proverbs 31:30

Satan would love for me, and my daughters, to take our eyes off Christ and stare adoringly in the mirror for hours.

What better idol is there than *me?* And, if I have enough beauty, I can get other people to worship me too. Two idols for the price of one. After all, according to the late Whitney Houston… *"the greatest love of all is inside of me."*

The greatest love of all is **not** inside of you or me. The greatest love of all is the love of God.

We must teach our daughters that God doesn't want women to be more *beautiful*. He wants them to be more like *Him*.

As a woman seeking after God's own heart, beauty is not the end goal, *holiness* is. Holiness in us brings glory to God. Yet, how much time do we spend focused on our *vanity* every day verses focused on our *holiness*? Beauty is not the goal, *holiness* is.

"Environments that emphasize holiness as a part of good faith will help create a new generation of disciples with deep-rooted faith." [107]
–David Kinnaman and Gabe Lyons, *Good Faith*

He has saved us and called us to a holy life—not because of anything we have done but because of his own purpose and grace.
2 Timothy 1:9

As Christian parents, what are we modeling to our daughters about beauty? Are we putting vanity in a higher place than it deserves?

Fact Check: Do older people have less value?

Is not wisdom found among the aged?
Does not long life bring understanding?
Job 12:12

In the early days of our country, young people respected and looked up to their elders. Older people were seen as valuable because of their wisdom and experience.

However, sometime during the Baby Boomer generation, people started trying to reclaim their youth. [108] Everything has become about looking and acting younger. This shift in attitude has escalated to a worship of youth.

Experience, wisdom, and perseverance should be celebrated. Youth is just a way to get experience, wisdom, and perseverance. And in our youth, we aren't done cooking yet.

The difference between the knowledge I currently have and what I knew twenty years ago is great. I am much wiser, more confident, and I know God at a deeper level. I would never go back to my twenties.

Are we perpetuating the lie to future generations that only young people have value by obsessing over youth?

Fact Check: Are celebrities on a higher plane than the rest of us?

We would probably answer this question, "of course not!" However, do our lives and attitudes reflect truth and a focus on what is real? Or, does our attitude reflect a worship of celebrity?

> *There is neither Jew nor Gentile, neither slave nor free, nor is there male and female, for you are all one in Christ Jesus.*
> Galatians 3:28

Does our life reflect an attitude of worship of rich and famous people? How much time are we spending reading People Magazine or watching reality TV shows?

We must be careful what shows our kids see us watching. From *The Kardashians,* to *The Real Housewives of (fill in the blank),* these types of "reality" shows *(an oxymoron)* only confuse kids because what they portray is *not* reality. And shows like *Shark Tank,* and *The Bachelor* idolize celebrity, beauty, and money.

Our kids will pick up on our values more by what we do and how we spend our time than by what we say. Our lifestyles reflect our values.

Most Christians know that these messages put out by the media are not true. But, God asks us not only to know the truth, but to *live it.* We must connect our daily lives and attitudes with the truths of God's Word.

> *But you are a chosen people, a royal priesthood, a holy nation, God's special possession, that you may declare the praises of him who called you out of darkness into His wonderful light*
> 1 Peter 2:9

We must pursue Jesus. We must live a *Biblical worldview* over the American Dream. We must live as though we are God's special possession.

Looking at our own lives as followers of Christ, what beliefs do we really hold about societal issues? Pop culture? Television, or social media?

Do we obsess about our bodies? Are we enamored with the latest fashion or celebrity? What does our life show that we value? These are hard questions to answer but they greatly affect the impressionable faith of our kids.

Blessed?

"We are so blessed to have been born in this country," some say. But are we, really? Most of us have our physical needs met, and we are not oppressed by our government. But, are we really the blessed ones?

First, Jesus tells us in the Sermon on the Mount that the poor in spirit, those who mourn, and those who are meek are the blessed.

And second, we must remember what Jesus said about the rich.

It is easier for a camel to go through the eye of a needle than for someone who is rich to enter the kingdom of God.
Matthew 19:24

According to these Scriptures, does anything about living in America cause us to be blessed? It might be more accurate to say that we, who live in this country, have a greater challenge.

"The ultimate deception is that freedom can be found in chains."[109]
–David Kinnaman and Gabe Lyons, *Good Faith*

Are we in danger of losing our souls to the American Dream?

Recently my husband and I watched a movie about Steve Jobs. This movie displayed not only the opportunistic side of the American Dream, but the extremely dark side as well.

Steve Jobs started Apple computers from his parents' garage in 1975.[110] He was a flower child of the 60s and 70s who enjoyed "free love" and recreational drugs. He was pretty much self-centered most of his life. He even rejected a child that he fathered because he didn't want her.

He was also a genius. He was an arrogant, narcissistic genius.

Jobs spent his life building an empire for himself. As his company took off, he grew in power and wealth. And he was greatly admired for his success.

Job's closest colleague and co-founder of Apple, Steve Wozniak, left Apple after twenty years with the company. Here is a quote from Steve Wozniak's character in the movie, *Steve Jobs*.

> You are the beginning and end of your own world, Steve, and it's so small, so sad. It's gotta be lonely… and it doesn't end well for you, and I'm not sticking around to watch.

Wozniak painted a picture of a sad, pathetic man who spent his life pining for the wrong things. A man who ended up alone. Steve Jobs achieved the American Dream, no doubt about it. He was rich and powerful. And many people admired him.

> *You say, "I am rich; I have acquired wealth and do not need a thing." But you do not realize that you are wretched, pitiful, poor, blind and naked.*
> Revelation 3:17

———

If we choose to stay in the shallow waters of the American Dream, we will miss out on God's great adventure. We will never experience the vast oceans below. We will never see the beauty of the coral reef or experience the sweetness of dolphins and sea turtles. Or feel the gentle rhythm of the sea on our skin. We will never experience the freedom of swimming in the open waters, not bound by gravity. What freedom we would miss.

Of course, along with all of the beauty and adventure of the deep are dangers that lurk below. Sharks, sting rays, eels, and jellyfish dwell in the sea as well. They are a part of it.

Are we willing to risk everything to pursue God's dream for our lives? Are
we willing to "put out into deep water?"
Luke 5:4

We must teach our kids to trust the reality of God's truth over the American Dream. And we must define success in terms of our faith.

God does not call us to a glamorous, **American** life.
He calls us to a **holy** life.

Are we going to live for Christ or the American Dream? We can't do both. And *who* or *what* we live for is a powerful testimony to the next generation.

"Our faithful God won't leave in endless hibernation those of us who still
show a pulse for Him. He seeks to break into our awareness and restore our
vision. God can use a fresh dream to wake us up."[111]
–Beth Moore, *Children of the Day*

So, let us awake and be asleep no more! Let every eye open and every ear eagerly await the word of the Lord, for *He is good!* And His dream for us is better than anything we could dream or imagine.

Wake up, sleeper, rise from the dead, and Christ will shine on you.
Ephesians 5:14

Don't let your kids settle for the American Dream.

God's got a much bigger dream for you and me. And for our kids. An adventure awaits us if we choose to follow Him. It is full of ups and downs, joy and suffering, and love and sorrow. But mostly, it is full of *Him*. And there is nothing better.

"For I know the plans I have for you," declares the LORD, *"plans to prosper you and not to harm you, plans to give you hope and a future."*
Jeremiah 29:11

"It would seem that Our Lord finds our desires not too strong, but too weak… We are far too easily pleased."
–C.S. Lewis

Chapter 11

The Power of **No**

Do your best to add holy living to your faith. Then add to this a better understanding. As you have a better understanding, be able to say no when you need to. Do not give up.
1 Peter 1:5-7

How often do our kids hear *No*? How often were we told *No* by our parents? What about our parents when they were kids? Our grandparents? Each successive generation of parents has catered to their kids more and more. Sadly, the word *No* is slowly disappearing.

We are appalled at anyone who spanks their children. The mantra, "spare the rod, spoil the child" is no longer culturally acceptable. Even saying *No* at all is frowned upon.

What is the consequence of a society where it no longer acceptable to say *No* to our children?

Without ever hearing *Nos*, our kids aren't learning the lessons they should be learning. When this happens, their maturity is stunted. This is why there are a lot of young adults who can't hold jobs, can't stay married, and basically, can't cope with life.

Kids are living at home much later in life than they ever used to. Hayden Shaw writes in his book, *Generational IQ*, "Today, almost one in three (emerging adults) return home to live with Mom and Dad."[112]

Our culture emphasizes *feelings* instead of *truth*. We act on beliefs such as, "if it feels good it must be right," "conflict or disagreements are not okay," and, "I want my kids to be happy."

Feelings are unpredictable, inconsistent, and often unreliable. To allow our feelings to dictate our behavior or attitudes is like "letting the tail wag the dog." Feelings have their place, but God makes it clear in His Word that feelings are not to be trusted.

If we choose to parent based on the truth of God's Word, instead of feelings, sometimes we must tell our kids *No*.

If any of you lacks wisdom, you should ask God, who gives generously to all without finding fault, and it will be given to you.
James 1:5

Yes or No

Yes Man is a movie about a man, "Carl," who is played by Jim Carrey. Carl is a pathetic character at the beginning. He is lonely, sad, and says *No* to everything and everyone.

Sitting outside the bank where he works one afternoon, he bumps into a former colleague who drags him to a self-help seminar called, "Yes Man." He is inspired and commits to saying *Yes* to every decision he makes for an entire year.

He falls in love, is promoted in his job, and he tries many new things. And, *poof!* Just like that, everything in his life improves by the magic word, *Yes*.

Wouldn't it be great if everything turned out this way if we always said *Yes*? Unfortunately, our world doesn't work that way. While being open to new experiences is a good thing, if we say *Yes* to everything, we will likely end up alone, obese, sick, miserable, and an addict. We were created to exist with limits.

Without a doubt, the word, *No,* can be exponentially more powerful and transformative than the word, *Yes,* in our lives. A *No* can change a life and grow character more than any *Yes* ever could.

For adults, *Nos* come in many forms.

- *holding back from saying "I told you so"*
- *controlling emotions instead of letting them control you*
- *being kind to people who aren't kind to you*
- *holding back your desires and letting someone else have their way*
- *keeping the peace when you are attacked*

If we take an honest look as adults, our lives consist of mostly *Nos* and just a few *Yeses*.

In the morning on your way to work you pass Dunkin Donuts, you think about that luscious French cruller and your mouth starts to water, but you keep on driving. You go to your job every day that pays the bills even though you would much rather be a novelist. You take your kids to Kohl's because they need shoes for the wedding in December and you see a cute dress, but you don't buy it. It is evening and you want to sit down, relax, and watch a movie, but your teenager wants to talk, so you turn off the TV. Even being lactose intolerant can be a *No* if you love pizza or ice cream.

We need to take the negative connotation off of the word *No*. Saying *No* to ourselves can be a positive force in our lives. We, and our kids, have much to gain from the word *No*.

Hearing the word *No,* showing restraint, and experiencing disappointment, are all a necessary part of life. The extent to which we mature and grow our character is often directly related to the amount of *Nos* we allow in our lives.

"Most modern North American Christians have little imagination for self-denial...the thousands of marketing messages we receive every day reinforce the idea that we should deny ourselves nothing...but self-denial is essential to following Jesus."[113]

–David Kinnaman and Gabe Lyons, *Good Faith*

Four Reasons Kids Need to Hear *No*

Emily had knee surgery this summer. As they were putting the IV in, I gazed at her face. It hadn't changed since she was four years old. She was my sweet, freckle faced, beautiful girl. My girls are beautiful and precious. It's hard to believe that I could love anyone as much as I love them.

I held her hand as the nurse secured her IV. Within a few seconds her eyes rolled back in her head and she was making strange sounds with her mouth. Her body convulsed in shock. I thought she was having a seizure. The nurses ran in to attend to her. She turned pale and grabbed her chest. *What is happening?* I thought! Panic swept through my body as I caressed her forehead and tried to soothe her. It was terrifying. Emily's body seemed to be fighting something and I couldn't do anything to help her. *Jesus, please help my sweet Emily*, I prayed.

The episode was short and she quickly regained consciousness. Color returned to her face as sweat dripped off her brow. Even though the incident was short-lived, and she was fine, those twenty or thirty seconds felt like an eternity.

There is nothing more terrifying to a parent than to see your child unconscious and convulsing. I thought about how much I loved my girls, and how losing either one of them would end me *(it wouldn't—God is good)*. These girls are my lifeblood. They are my beating heart.

The intense love a parent has for a child is a beautiful part of life. Love makes life worth living.

The greatest job I have as a parent is loving my children. Sometimes it's easy and sometimes it's not. However, part of this love is setting limits and telling them *No*.

Kids need to experience limits, and *Nos*. Our kids can't always have everything they want. Disappointment is a natural part of life. Maturity can only come through a series of *Nos*.

There are four reasons kids need to hear *No*.

1. God, the Father, has said *No* to us

God does and always has said *No* to His children. In His perfect and gentle way, He sometimes denies us what we ask for. *Why?* Because we often ask for the wrong things, or what we ask for is not *His* will for our lives.

You ask and do not receive, because you ask amiss, that you may spend it
on your pleasures.
James 4:3

In fact, God says mostly *Nos* in the Bible except when referring to His love and promises about our future with Him. He does not hold these things back from us.

King David's deepest desire was denied him by God.

I had it in my heart to build a house of rest for the ark of the covenant of
the Lord, and for the footstool of our God, and had made preparations to
build it. But God said to me, "You shall not build a house for My name,
because you have been a man of war and have shed blood."
1 Chronicles 28:2-3

And David got himself into a lot of trouble when he coveted Bathsheba, sent for her, slept with her, and then had her husband murdered. It was all because he wouldn't say *No* to what he desired.

God said *No* to the apostle Paul, who I admire greatly for his wisdom and commitment to the Lord. He easily could have been prideful, but God said *No* to help Paul stay humble.

I was given a thorn in my flesh, a messenger of Satan, to torment me. Three
times I pleaded with the Lord to take it away from me. But he said to me,
"My grace is sufficient for you, for my power is made perfect in weakness."
2 Corinthians 12:8-9

Moses asked God to send someone else to bring the people out of Egypt.
His answer was, *No.*

"Pardon your servant, Lord. I have never been eloquent, neither in the past
nor since you have spoken to your servant. I am slow of speech and tongue."
The Lord said to him, "Who gave human beings their mouths? Who makes
them deaf or mute? Who gives them sight or makes them blind? Is it not I,
the Lord? Now go; I will help you speak and will teach you what to say."
Exodus 4:10-12

Asking for wrong things with wrong motives is what children do. And
often, that's what we do when we pray. God sometimes denies us good things
we ask for as well. In times like these, we must remind ourselves that, as the
saying goes, "Father knows best."

By example, God has shown us how to love our kids lavishly and say *No.*
Everything He does is for our good. Every *No* God gives us could be followed
with, "I have something better."

2. Saying *No* to our kids grows character

Not only should we say *No* to our children, but I would say that it is our
job to do so. Our job as parents *after* extreme amounts of unconditional love
is to foster character in our kids. We want our kids to develop characteristics
that resemble Christ, are pleasing to God, and will ultimately help them
succeed in life.

"Suffering is one of God's primary avenues of growth
and identity formation."[14]
—Kara Powell and Chap Clark, *Sticky Faith*

We want our kids to learn to work hard, be able to submit to a boss, provide for themselves, and sustain satisfying and healthy relationships. We want them to grow up to be mature, Godly adults.

Train up a child in the way he should go, and when he is old,
he will not depart from it.
Proverbs 22:6 (KJV)

Parenting is a balance of love and *Nos*. They must go together. Saying *No* to our kids allows them the greatest lessons of childhood. These lessons, more than any other, will grow a kid into a mature adult. Failing to withhold anything from our kids breeds entitlement, and entitled kids become entitled adults. Entitlement is the opposite of humility, which is what Christ modeled for us.

Even though I was raised in an affluent area, I didn't always get what I wanted as my classmates seemed to. Most of them got brand new cars when they turned sixteen. I, however, did not. My needs were met, but I was not spoiled.

How do I feel about that in hindsight?

I am grateful to my parents for saying *No.* I am a very thankful person, I have grown in wisdom, and I believe in hard work and sacrifice. While I felt deprived at the time, I am much better off.

What characteristics does hearing *No* develop in our children?

Self-control

As we lovingly say *No* to our kids, we are teaching them the fruit of the Spirit that is self-control. As we say *No* to ourselves, we are showing them that sometimes we must withhold from ourselves.

Self-control is not a popular concept these days. Americans are all about instant gratification. Just watch a half an hour of television, Netflix, or spend time on social media, and it is evident. The message is loud and clear: *We're Americans, we shouldn't be denied anything.*

This attitude is becoming more and more apparent in our society. Americans show almost no restraint anymore. And nothing is "off limits."

Self-control is a fruit of the spirit (Galatians 5:22-23). We must help our kids gain this quality despite the world around them.

Patience

If kids have to wait for things in life, then the fruit of patience will grow in them. Sometimes they must wait for days, months, or years, and sometimes they must wait until they are an adult. Waiting produces gratitude, perseverance, and patience.

Just as practice makes perfect, waiting produces patience.

See how the farmer waits for the land to yield its valuable crop, patiently waiting for the autumn and spring rains. You too, be patient and stand firm, because the Lord's coming is near.
James 5:7-8

My seventeen-year-old daughter needed a car the summer between her junior and senior year because she had a job. So, we decided to get a third car. My mom offered to sell us her car when she bought a new one. She gave us a great deal. And we knew how well she had taken care of it. But my mom wanted to wait a few months.

The girls whimpered and whined because they didn't want to wait. *Of course they didn't!*

"Why does she need to wait?" they protested. "Can you talk to her and see if she can do it sooner?"

I said, "no." I explained how Grams had been generous enough to give us a great deal on the car. We needed to just be patient and grateful that we will have this car at all.

It was a great lesson in patience. Waiting lent itself to a greater appreciation of the car when we got it.

Love

If we are at the center of everything, as humans, we cannot thrive. God made us this way. We need *Him* at the center.

When kids are constantly catered to, they believe the world revolves around them. These kids have a rude awakening when they go out in the real world. The world will not coddle them. Being told *No* and experiencing disappointment teaches kids that it's not all about *them*. This truth frees them to look outside of themselves and to love as Christ commands us to.

If we teach our children that they are not the center of the universe, but *God* is, they are more likely to focus on loving others instead of only loving themselves.

> *And now these three remain: faith, hope, and love.*
> *But the greatest of these is love.*
> 1 Corinthians 13:13

As we talked about in Chapter 6, love is everything. One of our most important jobs as Christian parents is to teach our kids to love others well.

We must teach our kids to turn their focus outward, on others. Our kids must learn to love others. *Nos* can teach them this lesson.

Gratitude

Requiring our kids to wait for things encourages a thankful attitude. When they learn that nobody owes them anything, they are more likely to appreciate what they have.

There isn't anything that will ever be done for us that is greater than what God has already done. And there is no one who loves us more. *Gratitude* is the beginning of our response to God's amazing goodness and grace.

The sting of death is sin, and the power of sin is the law. But thanks be to God! He gives us the victory through our Lord Jesus Christ.
1 Corinthians 15:56-57

We all long for peace of mind, peace in our neighborhoods, peace in our families, and peace in the world. Jesus Christ offers us peace—His perfect peace. What more could we ask for in this life?

According to Priscilla Shirer, in her Bible Study, *The Armor of God*, "thanksgiving activates peace."[115] If we want to give our kids the gift of peace we must teach them gratitude.

Saying *No* to our kids can teach them to appreciate the *Yeses*.

3. Saying *No* to our kids gives them coping skills

Several years ago a boy in my daughter's middle school committed suicide. It shook our community to the core. It's devastating when young people take their lives before their brain is fully developed, and can thoroughly think through their options.

Emily was upset. We hugged, we cried, and we helped her process her feelings about her fallen classmate.

It's tragic the number of adolescents that are "lost." I was lost when I was a teenager, and a twenty-three year old friend of mine recently told me that she feels lost. She didn't know how to describe it any other way. My friend doesn't have faith. Without God, there is no foundation, no center. Without a compass it is tough to navigate life's rough waters.

Most kids today don't have coping skills. This is evidenced in the high number of school shootings we have witnessed in the past ten years, and the many teen suicides.

The most effective way to learn coping skills is to have to cope with something. Plain and simple. Our kids must experience rejection, disappointment, or a *No*. It is how they learn.

When trials come, life goes on whether we want it to or not. Regardless of our level of emotional distress, we still have to go to work or school the next day and fulfill our obligations and responsibilities. Saying *No* to our kids while surrounding them with love and support will likely cause them to be resilient.

We want our kids to grow up feeling worthy, loved, and confident because of our love and sacrifice. We also want our kids to grow up to be strong, physically and emotionally. Toughening our kids up emotionally while showering them in love will get the job done.

Adults, hopefully, have learned the skill of putting their feelings aside so they can function when needed. This skill can most affectively be learned through practice. And, the younger a person learns it, the better off they will be.

Sometimes in life we need to deal with pain alone. Over coddling kids keeps them from learning this skill.

- *How do I sit in the pain, yet, not let it destroy me?*
- *What do I do when the pain is so deep?*
- *How do I get up tomorrow morning and survive another day?*

These are questions all of us must answer in the midst of difficult times. They reflect a severity and intensity that hopefully, our children won't have to experience in childhood. The spectrum of the intensity of pain or discomfort will obviously vary from kid to kid. However, some situations kids face could prompt these questions.

We live in a fallen world. Therefore, many kids have a less than ideal childhood. Young people often are forced to deal with trauma.

- *divorce*
- *abuse*
- *loneliness*

These are examples of the sufferings of childhood. As parents, we surround our kids with love and support, but this can only carry them so far. Having practiced coping skills helps young people deal with these very difficult and unfortunate realities.

Teaching our kids coping skills is crucial.

As we talked about in Chapter 8, pain and tragedy are very real in our world. What we hope to give our kids is the ability to get up, dust themselves off, and get back in the game. We want to equip our children to handle anything that may come their way and persevere. Hearing *No* and having to cope with difficult things will get them there.

> *"Try to exclude the possibility of suffering and you find that you have excluded life itself."*
> —C.S. Lewis

4. Saying *No* to our kids teaches them to depend on God

About two years ago, Emily wanted a dog. We already had a dog and two cats at the time. I knew that introducing more stress in our lives would not be wise.

Our dog, Koda, has always been extremely mellow. We didn't even know if he could bark for the first six months we had him. He was calm, he didn't bark, he didn't jump, and he didn't require much effort or attention. God knew this was the dog we needed.

However, Emily wanted a dog that would be her best buddy. She wanted a dog that would follow her around and be playful. She wanted a dog that loved her and was loyal. But Koda was none of these things. He never caught a ball, cuddled up with anyone, waited for the kids at the bus stop, or comforted them in any way.

After much opposition, guilt, crying, begging and pleading, we ended up telling her *No*. There was no way we could have another dog. She was very upset. We hugged her and held her as she wept. It broke our hearts to see her this way.

It had been a really lonely year or two for her in the area of friendships. A close friend down the street decided that she didn't want to be friends anymore. We were also homeschooling at the time, which narrowed down her selection of friends. It was really tough for her. And it was hard for me to see her in pain and not jump in and save her from it. While I could love and support her, I couldn't give her the answer she wanted.

Eventually, Emily was back to her usual lively and delightful self. We were having dinner one night, and she talked about her loneliness. She said that she had been spending time with God and in the Bible when she was lonely or sad. Nothing could've thrilled me more than hearing those words from my child. She was learning to go to her Heavenly Father, the ultimate Source of comfort and love when she was down. There is no better place to go than to the One who loves us infinitely more than we could ever know.

Praise be to the God and Father of our Lord Jesus Christ, the Father of compassion and the God of all comfort, who comforts us in all our troubles.
2 Corinthians 1:3-4

Loneliness and disappointment, however unpleasant, can teach our kids to depend on God.

If we are always saving our kids, we are taking away the opportunity for them to know who their true savior is, Jesus Christ.

We need to teach our kids to go to God when they experience pain or despair. There is no better way than through a *No* or a disappointment. If they develop this practice early on, when they become adults and tragedy strikes, they will know who to turn to.

The Silent *No*

Hard work and sacrifice defined the children of WWI and WWII and the Great Depression, sometimes called *Builders, Traditionalists,* or the *Greatest Generation.*[116]

According to author Hayden Shaw, traditionalists "…cooperate, they serve with lower expectations than other generations, and they give generously."[117]

My grandparents were called the Greatest Generation because the values they held created a wonderful community dynamic. When people are loyal to each other and their country, work hard, and sacrifice for one another, families, communities, and nations thrive.

At the core of the Greatest Generation were *restraint* and *self-denial*, two values that this country has lost. These are what I call the "silent *Nos*."

Most of us know that we shouldn't fulfill our every desire, sometimes we must show restraint. There is power in the silent *No*. We must hold ourselves back to be obedient to Christ.

A silent *No* is like a diet. If we resist giving in to hunger, we can lose weight and feel better.

Turning your back on a sexual fantasy that does not fall within the bounds of your marriage is a silent *No*. Or, refusing to have an affair—even if your spouse has been neglecting you. Silent *Nos* can preserve families and marriages.

An alcoholic who has been sober for ten years and does not allow himself even one drink, is exhibiting a silent *No*—because he knows he can never have *just one*.

The silent *No* is like holding your tongue when your boss blames you for something unfairly. By keeping a cool head and avoiding an emotional reaction, you might earn a reputation of integrity.

My mom had a job for ten plus years working at the Internal Review Board office at a local hospital. It was a tough job. The IRB office dealt with grants that had a lot of confusing medical terms, and the doctors were often critical and demanding. My mom didn't like her boss and was frequently stressed and upset. But she persevered. She didn't quit.

After about five years, she was thoroughly confident in every detail of her job. When an opportunity to move to a different building away from the boss she disliked was presented, she took it and loved it. Because she stuck it out, and accepted a *silent No*, she finally had a job she loved.

Last year, Jessica didn't have very good friends at school. There was one in particular, who often criticized her. She'd say, "Why are you wearing a dress?," "You're too skinny," "You look awful without makeup," or, "Your hair looks weird." She just wasn't a nice kid.

When she'd come home from school and tell me what this girl said to her, my mind would flood with witty or snarky comebacks for her to throw back at her. Like, "Well, you're fat!," or, "At least I look good *with* makeup!"

But instead, I told Jessica that this girl is probably insecure, jealous, or hurt in some way. I gently remind her that we are to *love* our enemies. And in her context, this "friend" is a perfect example. I am teaching her to show restraint—even if she has been wronged.

In parenting, *silent Nos* are also required.

Parents have to restrain their protective impulses. Part of me would very much like to go down to the school and beat the snot out of kids who are mean to either of my daughters. But ultimately, my idea of justice has to be under the authority of God's justice.

Obedience to God's Word trumps our idea of justice.

Love First, *No* Second

Saying *No* to our children without a strong bond of love and acceptance in the relationship can be damaging. Kids need to be nurtured and have lavish amounts of love, hugs, and kisses. Kids need lots of encouragement, reminders of your love for them, and listening ears. They need to feel unconditionally loved every day.

Not only is love important to our children, but saying *No* to them would be ineffective without it.

God loves us every day and in every way. His love for us is scattered all over the Bible. He tells us that *His love endures forever* twenty-six times in one Psalm alone. He is our ultimate example of fatherly love.

The Lord your God is with you, the Mighty Warrior who saves. He will take great delight in you; in His love He will no longer rebuke you, but will rejoice over you with singing.
Zephaniah 3:17

God disciplines us as well. It's a part of love. We must also discipline our kids as part of loving them.

Love is why we say *No*. This kind of love is tough, but in Godly parenting, love and discipline go together. You can't have one without the other.

Chapter 12

Eleven False Mantras of Christian Parenting

Words are not mere words, you know. If they're not backed by a godly life, they accumulate as poison in the soul. Hymenaeus and Philetus are examples, throwing believers off stride and missing the truth by a mile.
2 Timothy 2:16-18 (MSG)

I t is Sally's birthday on Saturday and her mom is going to bake a cake. Her mom gets out the recipe for fish tacos and goes to the grocery store. After purchasing all of the ingredients from the recipe, she comes home to make her cake. She blends everything together in the food processor and pours the batter into the cake pan. After the oven preheats she slides the pan on the rack and sets the timer.

A half an hour later the house is filled with a putrid odor. She pulls the pan out of the oven and leaves it on the stove to cool. When she turns it over on the cake plate, it falls apart into a sticky, smelly mess.

What happened, she thought? I got all of the ingredients from the recipe and I followed the directions to a T.

We all know that we can't make a cake from a recipe for fish tacos. *At least not one I want to eat!*

Christian parents often use the wrong recipe when trying to foster faith in their kids. And the wrong directions combined with wrong ingredients will at the very least confuse our kids. Or worse, lead them away from the faith.

The messages we send to our kids, verbal or otherwise, are critical to the formation of their beliefs. In Chapter 5, we talked about being different than the world. We cannot use the same recipe as the world in raising our kids unless we want to produce worldly kids. We must use *God's* recipe.

The following are mantras that we in this country live by that may be leading our kids toward something other than faith in Christ.

False Mantra #1: Family comes first

"Family first" is a popular mantra in the Christian community. It sounds noble, right? Most people would agree that families are important. The health of families can make or break a nation.

However, in order for a family, community, or nation to thrive, *God* must come first.

I have often heard sermons in which the phrase "family first" is preached. And I've wondered, *do they realize what they are saying?*

No part of God's creation should ever come before *Him* in our lives, no matter how good or noble it seems.

God created families and uses them to raise up faithful workers for His Kingdom. The primary purpose of families is to spread the gospel and bring glory to God.

Family is important, but should never come first in our lives. That spot should always belong to God. He won't share His position with anyone or anything; not even our family.

If anyone comes to Me and does not hate father and mother, wife and children, brothers and sisters—yes, even their own life—such a person cannot be My disciple.
Luke 14:26

Let's dispel the notion that family is number one. Our kids must see that God always comes first.

False Mantra #2: Marriage comes first

Our marriages must come before many things; kids, jobs, friends, family. But our kids need to see that God comes before our marriages. They need to see that God comes before everything, *always.*

Along with our families, we can easily make our spouse or our marriage an idol. And most of the time, we will never see it. Marriage can be used as a substitute for God. Where do you get your needs met? Your spouse? Or, God?

"Marriage-centered marriages have become accepted and applauded rather than Christ-centered ones."[18]
–Francis Chan, *You and Me Forever*

While it is God's design that a husband and wife get joy from one another, our main source of joy, validation, and identity should come from God. *He* should be at the center of our marriages.

My husband and I have faced many challenges in our twenty-one years of marriage. Even though I couldn't love anyone on this earth more, it has not been easy. We would always see other couples who seemed to be in a marital-bliss bubble and wondered why we couldn't be like them.

Now when I see married couples who are infatuated with each other, I am almost sad for them. If my husband and I had not been forced to look to God for our worth and identity, would we have ever seen and experienced the intense presence of God as we have? If we were getting everything we desired from each other, would we be as in love with Jesus as we are now? Or would we have spent all of our energy being in love with each other?

Even though it has been difficult, we were forced to look to God for everything. It forced us to get our identity from Christ, *not each other*. It forced us to allow God to take His proper place in our life and in our marriage. We learned to get most of our contentment and joy from God, not from our spouse.

> *"Marriage is a good thing. But it's not an ultimate thing. Where the church has made marriage an idol—elevating it as the one relationship that will bring security, fulfillment, and intimacy—we need to think again."*[119]
> – David Kinnaman and Gabe Lyons, *Good Faith*

If God is not first or we lack a genuine connection with Him, our marriages will likely suffer. In times of marital strife, we must examine our relationship with God.

Most marital problems are essentially problems in our relationship with God.

If we are focusing solely on our marriage instead of God, we may not see the source of the problem. We end up blaming each other for our strife. Or, we spend hours in counseling, going to conferences, and reading self-help books looking for the solution to our marital woes.

God can use these resources to heal a marriage, but in and of themselves, they are insufficient. God is the great Healer—*of lives and of marriages*.

Marriage in Scripture is primarily introduced to show us the relationship between Christ and the church. It isn't about *us* or our marriages at all.

> *Let us rejoice and be glad and give him glory! For the wedding of the Lamb has come, and his bride has made herself ready…blessed are those who are invited to the wedding supper of the Lamb!*
> Revelation 19:7,9

We must realize and teach our children that it's not about us, or our marriages, it's all about *Him*.

False Mantra #3: Education and achievement come first

We often tell our children that their first priority as kids is to succeed in school. But is that true? Where in Scripture is that found?

While an education is important and school is their job, their first priority is to *God* and doing His will.

Jesus did not specify in His teachings that only adults needed to listen and obey Him. Nowhere did Christ set apart kids for a different purpose. They are tasked with loving God and one another, just as we are. The Great Commission is for people of all ages.

Education should not be first in our kids' lives. Even though we, as adults, have jobs, we serve God *first*.

Kids need to know that God comes before and above everything; above their education, above sports, and above clubs and activities. God comes first.

We emphasize education and achievement so much with our kids. They often top the list of priorities in our culture. We send our kids the message that academic excellence and being number one at a skill, are critical. Do we send them the message that praying and being in God's Word is critical?

The value of our kids' lives is not determined by how well they perform or what they achieve. Thank goodness success and achievement are not prerequisites for God's love and purposes.

Are we teaching our kids that God is more important than an education? Are we emphasizing the importance of keeping connected to *Him* more than excelling at a sport? Are we teaching our kids that knowing God's Word is more important than being a straight "A" student or being accepted into the best college?

How many of us sit at the kitchen table night after night helping our kids with homework? How many of us sit with our kids at night teaching them the Word of God?

We lobby for educational reform, campaign to be on the school board, and join the PTA. We stress about the degradation of our educational system in this country, and the poor condition of our schools. We worry about how China and other countries are blowing us away academically. It consumes us.

We have made education an idol in this country.

Sports and other activities can also be idols. How many American families run around every afternoon and evening carting kids to this activity or that sport? How many of us have our weekends tied up by games and tournaments—*even at the expense of church?*

Nowhere in Scripture does it say that getting an education or being the best at an activity or sport is the top priority for our kids. And it is a lot of pressure.

"Children over the last twenty-five years have internalized a fierce competitive sense… Trying to live up to those expectations is inherently stressful."[120]
–Tim Elmore, *Generation iY*

If we are faithful followers of Christ, we should be sharing Jesus' teaching with our kids more than teaching them math or science; more than teaching them to throw a baseball; more than teaching them to kick a football or hit a tennis ball; and more than teaching them to be successful and to achieve.

How do we help our kids put God first? We read Scripture with them. We teach them how to pray. We talk to them about God's way of handling the many situations they face throughout their day. Ask them if they are reading Scripture every morning. Encourage them to read the entire Bible in a year. Do it with them. We should be weaving God and His Word into our conversations every day, not just every once in a while.

Knowledge and skills are helpful and important for our kids to have. However, nothing comes before the knowledge of God. *Nothing.*

False Mantra #4: Make yourself happy first

My family's favorite TV show is ABC's, The *Middle*. Not just because we are Hoosiers and it takes place in Indiana, but because we see ourselves in the Hecks, the main characters.

My youngest daughter is definitely a mix of the characters of "Sue" and a little of "Brick"—she is bubbly, childlike, and a bit of a bookworm. My other daughter is a mixture of "Sue" and "Axl"—she is loyal, optimistic, and sweet as honey most of the time, but she can snark with best of them. And both my husband and I relate to the challenges of raising teenagers in middle class America.

One episode had a scene in which Frankie, the mom, and Sue were sitting on her bed, having a mother-daughter moment. Sue told her mom that a boy liked her. The advice Frankie gave her daughter was very telling of American culture today. She said, "Make yourself happy first."

Nowhere in Scripture does it talk about our *happiness*.

We need to be teaching our kids that their happiness should *not* come first. They need to lift up the name of Jesus, not their own. And put others before themselves.

> *For whoever wants to save their life will lose it, but whoever*
> *loses their life for me will find it.*
> Matthew 16:25

Kids will easily and naturally make themselves happy first. They are egocentric, so to them, living by this mantra will be as natural as eating or sleeping. They will easily accept the idea that the world revolves around them and their happiness.

Christian parents need to stress to their kids that the greatest love of all is the love of *God*, not the love of *themselves*.

False Mantra #5: Joining the rat race

You've got to love summer; the blue sky, the birds singing, the warm sun—*it's delicious!* Sometimes there is no substitute for the warm kiss of the sun on your skin. How glorious God's creation is!

One afternoon as I was taking a break from writing, I sat on my lounge chair on the patio. The warmth of the summer sun instantly brought me peace and relaxation. I turned over and laid on my stomach facing the ground. Looking closer at the cement bricks below, I noticed movement, like an ocean of red.

As I turned my head slowly to the left, the rest of the patio came alive. Thousands of little red dots, no bigger than the tip of my pen, scurried around going this way and that in a random array of motion. It was like tiny chickens with their heads cut off.

Have we become like little bugs, busying ourselves needlessly until we one day when we get stepped on? Often with no true purpose? Accomplishing nothing of lasting significance?

"The trouble with being in the rat race is that even if you win,
you're still a rat."[121]
–Lilly Tomlin

If we strip away everything in our life that is not eternal, how much is left? Is most of what we fill our days with of *eternal* importance? I know for my own life the answer is often, *probably not.*

Busyness can take the place of a Godly life. If every minute of our day is filled, how can we be available for the whispers of God? Only in still moments can our focus be completely on Him.

How many times have you heard someone say "I am so busy?" We have all felt stressed and pushed to the limit at one time or another. Whether it be a job that required insane hours, the intense pressures of school, or the rigors of raising a family.

Busyness is the disease of our time.
We are an overwhelmed and stressed out nation.

"There aren't enough hours in the day," we fret. The truth is, we all have exactly the same number of hours in the day as anyone ever had. Do you know of anyone who has more or less than twenty-four? How we spend them is up to *us*.

Did God intend for us to live life in a frantic state of continuous activity? Did He intend for our lives to be just a blur? Simply a means to an end?

Margin, the space that once existed between ourselves and our limits, is not a popular concept in American culture. [122] The lie is, if you have margin, then you are not keeping up.

How many of us take the time to sit at the feet of Jesus?

> *"Martha, Martha," the Lord answered, "you are worried and upset about many things, but few things are needed—or indeed only one. Mary has chosen what is better, and it will not be taken away from her."*
> Luke 10:41-42

We have made busyness an idol.

We talk about our multiple jobs and how busy we are. And we don't just talk about it, *we brag*. Christians, along with the rest of the world, wear their busyness like a badge of honor.

Busyness is one of Satan's most seductive tools.

- *busyness can feed our pride*
- *busyness can keep us from dealing with our "stuff"*
- *busyness can cause us to be self-reliant instead of dependent on God*
- *busyness can become a substitute for a Godly life*

This issue is crucial to the spiritual development of our kids. They won't hear His voice if they are never still. And if they don't learn this lesson while they live at home with their parents, it is unlikely they ever will. The world celebrates busyness.

Always have margin in your life. And, create and leave room for your kids to have margin as well. Leave space for God to move. Notice those around you. And always remember that God is number one and people are more important than our schedules.

False Mantra #6: Never show weakness

The View is a talk show that I happened to watch one day while I was doing my workout. Joy Behar, one of the hosts, opened the show with, "This is for those of you who support the vice president, all two of you…"

I thought to myself, *what possible dirt could she have on the vice president?* Mike Pence used to be our governor here in Indiana. And we Hoosiers are pretty mellow.

Apparently, on March 29th, 2017, Ashley Parker of the *Washington Post* tweeted the following. "Mike Pence never dines alone with a woman not his wife, nor does he attend events with alcohol, without her by his side."[123]

Behar proceeded to chastise him. "What is he afraid of?" she asked.

We all know what he's afraid of. Maybe if more politicians adopted a rule like this, there would be more time for legislation and improving our country, and less time spent on sex scandals.

I applaud Vice President Pence for his firm stand to protect his marriage. He is addressing a weakness that many men have by avoiding temptation.

True strength is found when we acknowledge our weakness.

When it comes down to it, it's not about our strength or our weakness. It's not about *us* at all. It's about *God's* strength and *His* power. The more weakness we surrender to the Lord, the more of His power He gives to us.

"It's not a matter of our equipment, but a matter of our poverty; not of what we bring with us, but of what God puts in us...God's friendship is with those who know their poverty, He can accomplish nothing with the person who thinks that he is of use to God."[124]
–Oswald Chambers, *My Utmost For His Highest*

The world tells us to value the strong and powerful. Yet, God says in 2 Corinthians 12:9, *"My grace is sufficient for you, for my power is made perfect in weakness."* God does great things with the foolish, the weak, the lowly, and the despised things of the world. He doesn't recruit only people who appear strong.

God chose the foolish things of the world to shame the wise; God chose the weak things of the world to shame the strong. God chose the lowly things of this world and the despised things—and the things that are not—to nullify the things that are, so that no one may boast before him.
1 Corinthians 1:27-29

I love the quote by Henry T. Blackaby, "The reality is that the Lord never calls the qualified; He qualifies the called." *Amen to that!*

You have to be the best at something. You must achieve and stand out in this world. You have to be strong to survive. These are messages of the world. They are lies.

Not only does this not coincide with the teachings of Christ, but it can put unnecessary pressure on our kids. Some of us in life will be the best at something. Most of us will not.

Kids believe they must be the best quarterback, the strongest soccer player, or the fastest runner. They feel pressure from parents to be the best singer, piano player, or the star of the show. They must make the best teams, or the most elite groups.

What does Jesus command us to do in this life? Be the star athlete? Get the lead in the play? Win trophies? Be lifted up and admired by those around us?

Jesus tells us to love abundantly, serve the poor generously, and spread the gospel passionately.

We must ask ourselves who do we want to glorify, ourselves, or God? And, who are we teaching our kids to glorify?

Each of us has a weakness that makes us need a savior. I know I seriously fall short. I can't quite seal the deal on my own. No one can.

Weaknesses are not a bad thing. We all have them. We must teach our kids that it is okay to have weaknesses, because in *Him* we are strong.

False Mantra #7: It's none of my business

...I sensed something was wrong with the Smiths next door, but I didn't want to intrude.

....Jackie at the office seemed upset today, but I didn't want to pry.

...I heard that Kaylie's parents just got a divorce, but it's none of my business.

...It feels like Jeff is walking away from the Lord, but I don't want to meddle.

In American society, we like to appear as though we have it all together. We all wear our masks. And we live very separate lives.

God did not create us to have "our own business." He created us to need each other. He created us to be the body of Christ; one body. The early church was all about unity and getting in each other's business.

We must not only care for the physical needs of others, but spiritual needs as well. If one person in a community of believers is entangled in sin, than it is up to the body of believers to help them.

> *Brothers and sisters, if someone is caught in a sin, you who live by the Spirit should restore that person gently.*
> Galatians 6:1

Let's get involved, let's pry, and let's make it our business. Let's go outside of our comfort zone for the sake of our brother. We must stop ignoring the elephant in the room and get down to business.

If one of you should wander from the truth and someone should bring that person back, remember this: Whoever turns a sinner from the error of their way will save them from death and cover over a multitude of sins.
James 5:19-20

False Mantra #8 You can have it all

A friend was struggling between ambition and family relationships. He and his wife have a four-year-old daughter and a baby. Let's call my friend Max.

Max had lofty career goals. He was offered an impressive salary right out of graduate school from a prestigious consulting company.

His job required that he travel Monday through Thursday every week. During his last project that was out of town, he noticed his relationship with his four-year-old was suffering. Max wasn't home very much, and when he was, he felt like he was constantly disciplining her. They were having very little positive daddy-daughter time. So, he requested to be put on a local project, and their relationship improved.

When it comes to spending time with our kids, it's not just **quality** time that counts. It takes **quantity** to get to **quality**.

Max's next project was in Paris. It would come with a promotion and a hefty pay increase. It was the chance of a lifetime and he couldn't pass it up.

So Max went. And he traveled again, and again.

He had already witnessed with his daughter that he couldn't have it all. She suffered when she didn't see daddy for long periods of time. However, in his mind, the payoff was too great.

Let's look at another family. Let's call them Jack and Diane.

Jack works at a consulting company. Diane is a PhD and teaches at the university. They have two adolescent boys and live in a trendy neighborhood in the city. Most of their money is tied up in their house, and Diane likes to shop for new clothes, new furniture, and new cars. Their lifestyle requires both of their impressive incomes.

The oldest son, a teenager, is having difficulty in school. He doesn't quite fit in and is having a hard time making friends. He is bullied at school and doesn't feel like his parents listen to him. Most alarming, though, is he recently threatened suicide.

A threat of suicide should never be taken lightly. If a kid is getting bullied at school and it is affecting him enough to threaten suicide, drastic measures must be taken.

Are we willing as parents to do whatever it takes to help our children?

For Jack and Diane this may mean that one of them quits their job and homeschools their troubled son. Or, they may need to move so their son can go to a different school and have a fresh start.

Parents are often unwilling to go this far. We reap what we sow. Or, our kids reap what we sow. If we are unwilling to sacrifice for our children, they will likely suffer. I don't see a lot of parents sacrificing *for* their children today. Sadly, kids end up being collateral damage.

The mantra, "You can have it all," is a lie. How do we figure we can do an infinite number of things with a finite amount of time, energy, and money? It just doesn't make sense.

You can't have it all when you are a parent—at least not without something or *someone* being sacrificed.

False Mantra #9: Store up treasures on earth

A missionary friend of mine is turning forty this year. She has spent much of her adult life on the mission field in Africa, serving the nationals.

Raising enough support for her meager salary and covering her expenses for the ministry was hard enough. Retirement savings was just not on her radar.

I can imagine the reaction some people would have to someone who is forty not having retirement savings. Someone might say, "You haven't started saving for retirement yet?" followed by an awkward silence. Or, "Wow, you'd better get going, you're way behind," or, "How irresponsible."

Any book on personal finances would sound the alarm on someone who has not saved for retirement.

However, retirement savings or any savings for that matter is "storing up treasures" for yourself on earth. Is saving money not treasure? And who are we saving it for, if not for ourselves?

My point is not to say that 401ks or IRAs or any savings accounts are wrong. I am not saying that we should never save. I'm not saying that having a retirement fund is bad. However, I am saying that we need to see things for what they really are. Let's call a spade, a spade. Saving money is storing up treasures on earth. The two are the same. So we have to be careful.

*Command them to do good, to be rich in good deeds, and to be generous
and willing to share.*
1 Timothy 6:18

We would never call someone out because they hadn't sold everything to follow Christ, or because they have never gone on a mission trip, or because they weren't giving to the poor. Yet, we look down on people who haven't saved for retirement.

We must teach our kids Biblical principles about money over culturally accepted principles. We, as Christian parents, must train their minds on the things above (Colossians 3:2). We must teach them to view things through the eyes of eternity.

Are we allowing room in our finances to let God stretch us? Do our kids see us being generous with our money? Are we trusting *Him* with our financial future?

"Bring the whole tithe into the storehouse, that there may be food in my house. Test me in this," says the LORD Almighty, "and see if I will not throw open the floodgates of heaven and pour out so much blessing that there will not be room enough to store it."
Malachi 3:10

The eyes of our children are on us when it comes to money. What are we teaching them?

False Mantra #10: You have the right to fight for yourself

The world we live in is unjust. Every time my girls say "it isn't fair!" I gently remind them that the world is not fair, but our Heavenly Father is.

In another episode of *The Middle*, the parents, Frankie and Mike tell their daughter, "You've got to stand up and fight for what's yours."

What does God say about injustices done to us? What does God say about our "rights?"

Do not resist an evil person. If anyone slaps you on the right cheek, turn to them the other cheek also. And if anyone wants to sue you and take your shirt, hand over your coat as well.
Matthew 5:39-40

What does God say about us being just toward others?

Learn to do right; seek justice. Defend the oppressed. Take up the cause of the fatherless; plead the case of the widow.
Isaiah 1:17

We must fight for others, but not fight for ourselves, or our reputation— unless it brings *God* glory. But we can be comforted knowing that eternity is perfectly just because God is perfectly just. We will all get what is coming to us in eternity.

God is just: He will pay back trouble to those who trouble you and give relief to you who are troubled, and to us as well...He will punish those who do not know God and do not obey the gospel of our Lord Jesus.
2 Thessalonians 1:6-8

"We teach that even though Jesus allowed His rights to be trampled, we should fight for ours. We teach that even though Jesus lived simply, we have the right to live luxuriously. Even as we teach that Jesus was rejected by the world, we pursue popularity."[125]
−Francis Chan, *You and Me Forever*

False Mantra #11: It is the church's job to pass on faith to the next generation

Most Christian parents would never speak these words or even think it consciously. However, are we living as if it is *our* job to pass on our faith?

Hands down, youth pastors have the most difficult job in the church. Coming alongside teenagers in their spiritual walk is challenging and often frustrating. We, as parents, know that dealing with teenagers is not easy. They can be a wrecking ball of hormones and emotions.

As a parent of teens in the church, I want to say an enormous *thank you* to all youth ministers and pastors and youth leaders. They have an awesome responsibility. A lot is put on their shoulders by parents and the church leadership. And much of it doesn't belong there.

The responsibility of passing on the faith to young people lies with parents. Period.

If we as Christian parents leave the development of the faith of our kids solely to our churches, then they will continue to walk away from the faith. If we do not step up as parents, the faith of our kids and future generations will suffer.

Chapter 13

Actionable Intelligence

"History repeatedly has demonstrated that inferior forces can win when leaders are armed with accurate intelligence."[126]
–Gregory Elder, Defense Intelligence Agency (DIA)

According to Collins Dictionary, *actionable intelligence is* "the necessary background information that will enable someone to deal quickly and efficiently with a particular situation."[127]

We talked about the fact that *who* we are is the most powerful influence when passing on our faith to our kids. However, we must have ideas to put into action. What are some habits we can help our kids form right now? What are some tools we can give them that will foster growth in their faith?

Just Read It!

My natural tendency is to be a *Mary* and sit at the feet of Jesus. I have less *Martha* in me than I would care to admit. If you saw my house, you would agree with me.

I am hungry for God's Word. And I am starting to see it for what it really is—the living, breathing, Word of God. It is a gift, a love letter, a mirror, an admonition, and a glimpse into our future with Him.

> *When your words came, I ate them; they were my joy and my heart's delight, for I bear your name, Lord God Almighty.*
> Jeremiah 15:16

However, most kids never read the Bible before they leave home.

> By the time the average child leaves for college at age eighteen, he or she will have never read the entire Bible (which can be read cover to cover in about eighty hours), and many will never have opened a Bible.[128]

As I thought about getting the Word of God into my kids, I was overwhelmed at the prospect. Time was running short.

> *"The best way for young people to learn about Christ is through the Scriptures. That's the only way I have found for any of us to truly grasp the exclusivity of Christ's message."*[129]
> –David Kinnaman, *You Lost Me*

Question: How do we get the Word of God into our children?
Answer: They have to read the Bible for themselves.

> *Keep this Book of the Law always on your lips; meditate on it day and night, so that you may be careful to do everything written in it.*
> Joshua 1:8

I can't make my girls fall in love with Scripture. And, that's okay. My job is to teach them to read God's Word and encourage them to *do* what it says.

How do we create the best chance for our kids to develop a lifelong love of Christ? We introduce them to Him. We show them who He is. Jesus Christ is most powerfully revealed in Scripture.

Having your kids read the Bible might be more valuable than going to church, participating in youth groups, and attending camps and conferences. Spending time with God and being in His Word is likely to have more impact on their faith than anything else.

> "...those families who hold the highest view of Scripture seem to have the best rates of faith transference to their children."[30]
> —David Kinnaman, *You Lost Me*

How many of us send our kids to various church activities, but never emphasize the importance of reading the Bible?

If we get our kids into the Word of God, the Word of God will get into our kids.

> *Then we will no longer be infants, tossed back and forth by the waves, and blown here and there by every wind of teaching and by the cunning and craftiness of people in their deceitful scheming. Instead, speaking the truth in love, we will grow to become in every respect the mature body of him who is the head, that is, Christ."*
> Ephesians 4:14-15

If we get our kids into the Word of God, the Word of God will get into our kids.

Bible studies, commentaries, and other books on Scripture are available to help us unpack the amazing complexities of the Word of God. I have used many and been blessed by them. But they must not be a substitute for our kids actually reading the Bible for themselves. Everything they need to live a godly life is in there.

> *His divine power has given us everything we need for a godly life through*
> *our knowledge of him who called us by his own glory and goodness.*
> 2 Peter 1:3

Nothing can take the place of actually reading the Bible word for word. Anyone over the age of twelve can read the Bible for themselves, and have enough understanding to do what it says.

Our kids should start with the gospels, which are the most important part of Scripture for them to know. The gospel message is what our faith is all about.

JD Greear writes in his book, *Gospel*, that you should "…see the gospel not only as the means by which you get into heaven, but as the driving force behind every single moment of your life."[131]

Our kids must know the story of how we have been redeemed by the blood of Christ. It is crucial they know what Jesus said. The rest of the New Testament comes next—the apostles teaching and the early church. Then they can go on to tackle the Old Testament.

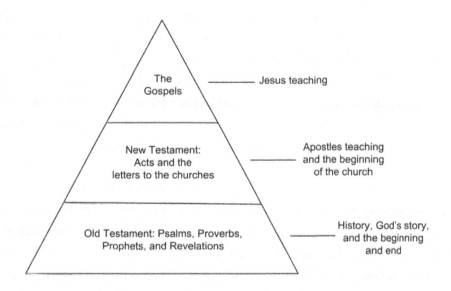

Challenge: Challenge your teen to spend equal amounts of time watching TV and using their devices as reading the Bible for a couple of weeks. To minimize the groans and protests, maybe offer them a reward, maybe even money. Don't think of it as a bribe, think of it as *leverage*. Any way we can get our kids into the Word of God is a step toward building their faith.

"Nothing threatens the enemy more than a believer with the Word of God living and active on her tongue."[132]
–Beth Moore, *Believing God*

Serving And Sacrifice

My stepfather, John, was diagnosed with cancer in February of 2009 and passed away the following October.

Cancer is a nasty thing. Those who have gone through it, whether directly, or as a caregiver, know that it can be the truest test of character—*in the patient and in the care-givers.*

John went into the hospital in August and never came home.

My mom was his primary caregiver. And I supported them both as much as I could. I was at the hospital with John when she couldn't be or when she needed a break. I was often there with both of them.

I quickly became overwhelmed physically and emotionally. The girls were seven and nine, and my mom was living with us at the time. I also was homeschooling. Between taking care of the kids and the house and being at the hospital as much as I could, I was exhausted. Not to mention the emotional fatigue I was experiencing.

John and I had always had a strained relationship. He had a bad relationship with a stepdaughter in a previous marriage. With him bringing baggage into the relationship and me being a teenager and coping with the loss of my family, we never had a chance.

It's a strange thing taking care of someone who was an adversary for so many years. It doesn't come naturally. It is a *divine nature* kind of thing. I had to tap into that. I had to depend on the Holy Spirit to make me better than I was, better than I could be. I wasn't capable of loving this man. Not after our long and painful history. Not after everything we'd been through.

However, God is always able, and we only have to be willing.

John needed love. He was facing his own mortality, which nobody should go through alone.

Sometimes we need to just say, "I got nothing, Lord," and recognize our inadequacy—our *not-God-ness*.

Sometimes all we have to do is show up, and God will do the rest.

I have great admiration for the men and women of the armed forces. Their willingness to volunteer for some of the most dangerous, exhausting jobs on the planet is extraordinary. They sacrifice so much. This sacrifice is their greatest value to our country, much more than what they actually *do* for us.

God wants an army of soldiers who are willing to show up for battle. They don't have to be the strongest or the most agile. They just have to be willing to show up.

Showing our kids the importance of loving God through service and sacrifice is paramount to passing on our faith. Whether it is helping a family member or someone in the community during a difficult time, serving at a shelter, or another avenue of serving, we must have them start serving as young as possible.

"Many of the deepest truths of Christianity become clear when we put our faith into action; in the doing, believing makes sense."[133]
–David Kinnaman, *You Lost Me*

Challenge: Try various areas of serving in the community with your kids. Pick out a family member that is elderly or isolated and encourage your kids to reach out to them and offer them assistance. Work with your kids on loving the difficult people in their life.

It Takes a Village

In recent years, new challenges have arisen with parenting our girls. As they have become young women, more serious and impactful issues have come up. They are making decisions that can affect the rest of their lives. At the same time, I can no longer keep them under my wing. I must start to let them go.

It takes a village to raise kids. No doubt about it. Raising kids is the toughest job that any of us will ever have. And God never intended for us to do it alone.

God has given us reinforcements in parenting. It's called *community*. We were never meant to raise our kids in isolation. Kids will benefit more from having other Godly adults speaking truth into their lives, than having input only from parents.

Every kid growing up in the church needs a mentor.

"Our lives build on the faithfulness of the believing generations before us."[134]
– Beth Moore, *Believing God*

When I was a teenager, dealing with my parents' divorce and adjusting to new stepfamilies overwhelmed me. I was very much lost.

God placed a mentor in my life in a time of great turmoil. Deb was a youth leader at my church who took me under her wing. Deb spent one-on-one time with me for years, loving me and speaking truth into my life when I felt very alone. I don't know how I would have survived those years without her.

Everyone needs an advocate in life. Unfortunately, parents often become less of an advocate for their kids when they get divorced and start new families.

Deb is still a mentor to me today. Though a thousand miles separate us, our bond in Christ never fails. Deb has been supporting and loving me through the ups and downs of life. She is a little farther down the road in life and faith. I am so grateful that God brought her into my life. Her wisdom and spiritual depth has been a blessing.

Knowing how beneficial this relationship has been for me, I started looking for mentors for my daughters. I knew that having a voice speaking into their lives and encouraging their faith other than mine and my husband's would be powerful for their faith in Christ. However, I must admit finding someone who loves well, had the time to pour into my kids, and passionately followed Christ, wasn't easy.

Being available to the youth of the church is one of many reasons we need to leave margin in our lives. If we are too busy, kids will fall through the cracks. Too many young people are leaving the church without any adults ever reaching out to them.

> *"Kids experience Jesus Christ when adults in the church give them grace, time, and genuine love with no hidden agenda...Most kids lack connection to and investment from a church community that is mobilized to reach them"*[35]
> —John Ortberg and Jim Candy

What is the modus operandi of a mentor? We must look for adults who have a strong faith, who love our kids, and ideally, have a connection with them. A coach, a Sunday school teacher, a youth leader, a neighbor, a grandparent, parents of our kid's friends, and seniors in the church are a good place to start.

I had someone in mind for my youngest daughter. She was loving and cared about her. She was retired and had the time. And she was a great listener. She was perfect, *except*, she was not a follower of Christ. And that was a deal breaker. We must find *Godly* mentors for our kids if we want to encourage a lifelong faith in them. Mentors must be more than just good role models.

We must find Godly mentors for our kids if we want to encourage a lifelong faith in them. Godly mentors are more than just good role models.

Challenge: Find a mentor for each of your kids. Someone who can build a relationship with your child, someone who listens well, and will ultimately point him or her to Christ. Contribute to the relationship by giving them a Starbuck's gift card to use while meeting with your child.

The Power of Purpose

The Purpose Driven Life by Rick Warren topped the Wall Street Journal best seller charts as well as Publishers Weekly charts with more than thirty million copies sold by 2007. It was also on the New York Times Bestseller list for more than ninety weeks.[136]

It seemed like it found its way into every Christian home, Bible study and church in the country. Why did this message resonate with so many people? As human beings, we long for purpose and meaning in our life.

Several months ago I watched a debate between William Lane Craig and Christopher DiCarlo. The topic was *Does God Matter?* I was intrigued.

God absolutely does matter. Nothing good would exist without Him. The reason goodness, love, mercy, morality, and purpose exist in the world, is because God put it there.

We couldn't have purpose without God, and we couldn't live without purpose. Therefore, God matters very much.

There isn't one human being on the planet that doesn't have or need purpose in their life. It is what separates us from the animals. We have a soul and therefore, we search for purpose and meaning.

Human beings are *why* creatures. We not only seek to know what, and how things work, but also, *why*. We want to know there is a reason. We need there to be something greater than ourselves. It's how God created us.

Loren Eiseley, an American anthropologist, educator, philosopher, and natural science writer said, "Man is the cosmic orphan. He's the only creature in the universe that asks why."

According to Nancy Fitzgerald, and the Anchorsaway Worldview Curriculum, everyone has five life questions.[137] They all seem to echo the *whys* that haunt us.

1. From where did I come?...*why am I here?*
2. Why is there such a mess in the world?...*why am I here?*
3. Is there any hope?...*why am I here?*
4. What is my purpose in life?...*why am I here?*
5. What happens when I die?...*why am I here?*

Why are we here? We must have an answer.

Did your kids go through the annoying *why* phase when they were toddlers? It didn't matter what answer you gave them, they still wanted to know *why*? It is human nature.

The *whys* express our need for purpose.

Our kids were made for a divine purpose. We must help them find it.

We must not neglect to do this because they are young. Many significant characters in the Bible were young. Jeremiah was a youth, and Jesus' beloved disciple, John, was thought to be young as well.

> *But the LORD said to me, "Do not say, 'I am too young.' You must go to everyone I send you to and say whatever I command you.*
> Jeremiah 1:7

There is nothing more powerful than a
young person with purpose.

Challenge: Help your kids serve in many different areas. Expose them to many different people and places. Pray that their spiritual gifts and purpose would be revealed to them.

Chapter 14

Apologetics and Worldviews

But in your hearts revere Christ as Lord. Always be prepared to give an answer to everyone who asks you to give the reason for the hope that you have. But do this with gentleness and respect.

1 Peter 3:15

"For the next generation, the lines between right and wrong, between truth and error, between Christian influence and cultural accommodation are increasingly blurred."[38]

–David Kinnaman, *You Lost Me*

A couple summers ago a Mormon temple was built just down the road from my house. They were giving tours, so my family and I decided to go. We waited in line and then were herded into a small room to watch a video. The whole thing reminded me of Disney World. The young hosts were extremely happy, friendly, and well trained. It felt as if we were getting on the boat ride at "It's a Small World After All."

After twenty minutes of beautiful people attempting to convince us that becoming Mormon would bring us happiness forever, we proceeded to the temple for our tour. Happy people with huge smiles on their faces were at every turn.

The temple was visually stunning. There were marble floors and gold painted ceilings. The walls were decorated with beautiful, one-of-a-kind paintings of Jesus Christ. And the baptistery looked like something out of a movie. It was quite a spectacle!

As the tour wrapped up, we were directed into a tent, as if we were getting off the ride and exiting through the gift shop. Inside were missionaries who answered questions and handed out literature on Mormonism. I couldn't believe how many times I saw the word *happy*, or *happiness* on the many displays that lined the tent. Wow! A faith that promises happiness? Who wouldn't want that?

The thought hit me, if our kids are not mature in their faith, they can fall prey to cults, such as Mormonism. The big smiles and promises of peace and happiness are unquestionably attractive.

The Mormon missionaries will say they are Christians, but they are not. As I studied their beliefs and practices, a noticeable pattern emerged. The specifics of Mormonism bring God lower, while man is lifted up until he is eventually a god.[139] It's simply ridiculous to call this Christianity.

We must equip our kids to spot false teaching. And they need to be aware of what sort of cults and religions they might encounter.

When you hear the word *apologetics*, you may immediately think of atheism. Oh, if this were the only worldview to compete with! According to Wikipedia there are approximately forty-two hundred religions in the world.[140]

Christianity is one religion out of thousands. How will our kids know if Christianity is the truth if we don't show them?

Christian kids may encounter these types of questions and accusations.

• *If God is good, why is there so much suffering in the world?*

- *Why do you believe in God when there isn't any evidence of him?*
- *You're a Christian? I thought you were smart!*
- *How can you believe that Christianity is the only right way? How close-minded and intolerant!*

How our kids respond to these questions and statements reflect the confidence they have in their faith. Apologetics can equip them with answers.

Apologetics

Apologetics is a powerful tool that should be in every thinking Christian's toolbox. The word *apologetics* comes from the Greek word ἀπολογία (apología) meaning "a speech in defense." The Greek term refers to a reasoned defense that would be given in a court of law.[141]

When applied to Christianity, apologetics is simply *reasoned arguments in defense of the Christian worldview.* Apologetics doesn't necessarily start with the Bible; rather, it starts with evidence we see in nature, using philosophy and arguments to deduce the probability that there is a God.

Apologetics does not try to replace truths that are revealed in the Bible, nor does it undermine the inner-witness of the Holy Spirit. We can *know* the truth of Christianity without apologetics. However, it is a powerful way to *show* others the truth of Christianity. By removing intellectual barriers, people might be more open to the Christian worldview.

What do our kids need to know to be able to give a reasoned defense for their faith? They need to be able to answer these five questions.

1. What is truth?
2. Why do I believe God exists?
3. Why do I believe Jesus is the Son of God?
4. Why do I believe the Bible is true?
5. How does being a Christian affect my life?

1. What is Truth?

Frank Turek and Norman L. Geisler in their book, *I Don't Have Enough Faith to be an Atheist,* claim that "truth is a casualty of our popular culture. And when truth goes, the authority of the gospel is undermined."[142]

Believing in truth is essential to a strong, healthy faith.

According to dictionary.com, *truth* is the true or actual state of a matter, or, a proven or verified principle or statement. If truth is proven and verified, it is absolute.

Truth is not relative.

Think about it: if truth is relative, why should our kids go to school? If they can just decide their own truth, than what is the point of learning math, science, or history? Without objective, absolute, truth, nothing they learn in school is relevant to anyone except the person teaching it.

Our entire civilization is run by the objective truth of numbers. We count on numbers for finances, temperature, speed, time, grades, taxes, etc. If we didn't agree on a set of objective truths about numbers, our society could not function.

Truth, by its very nature is *exclusive*. If something is true, it means that contradictory statements are necessarily false. Nobody doubts this when it comes to the hard sciences; people believe that the statement "gravity exists" is objectively true, and that the statement "gravity does not exist" is objectively false. But, when it comes to religion and worldviews, people have no problem saying "Christianity may be true for you, but it's not true for me."

However, truth is objective, meaning, it is attached to the *object*, and it is therefore unchanging. What people are claiming today is that truth is subjective, meaning, it is attached to the *subject*. They claim for each individual person, or *subject*, there may be a different truth.

For example, take the sentence "Doug caught the red ball." In this sentence, Doug is the subject, and the ball is the object. There is an inherent truth about the ball—*the ball is red*. It makes no difference what Doug, the subject of the sentence, believes the color of the ball to be. Doug might sincerely believe the ball is blue, but that does not change the fact that *the ball is red*. The subject's beliefs are irrelevant to objective truths.

Religion is perceived as something that helps one get through life; and if that indeed is its purpose, then of course each person will have their own religious beliefs that are useful to them. It can be likened to a therapy session; in order to help a patient, the counselor tailors the session to the subject they are counseling.

It is this misperception of religion that has led so many people to believe in the relative truth of religious worldviews, rather than in absolute truth. One of the most critical lessons we need to teach our kids is that absolute truth can be applied to religion as much as it is applied to chemistry, economics, and mathematics.

Religion is not a matter of opinion, convenience, or utility. It is an objective reality of the universe.

There is one set of facts about God and the universe that is objectively true. Any view that doesn't correspond to these truths is necessarily false.

There is *one* view of attaining salvation that is objectively true; all other views are false. There is *one* view of the spiritual world that is objectively true. There is *one* view of our eternal destiny that is objectively true. There is *one* view of the origins of the universe that is objectively true. All views contrary to these truths are as false as the statement two plus two equals five.

To illustrate, consider common statements that we hear in our culture, and replace key terms with words of a different subject matter. Consider the following statement that I mentioned earlier:

How can you believe that Christianity is the only way? How close-minded and intolerant!

Now let's replace Christianity with, say, geography.

How can you believe that seventy-one percent of the earth is covered in water? How close-minded and intolerant!

Let's try mathematics.

How can you believe that eleven, seventeen, and twenty-nine are prime numbers? How close-minded and intolerant!

Let's try biology.

How can you believe that the heart pumps blood? How close-minded and intolerant!

These statements suddenly sound so absurd! When you accept that religious truths are just as objective as these other sciences, you realize there must be one true worldview. If there is one objectively true worldview, then all contrary worldviews must be false.

Determining which worldview is true is a different matter.

Which worldview is true? Maybe it is atheism, which believes there is no God. Maybe it is Hinduism, which believes there are 330 million gods. Maybe it is Mormonism, which believes that we can become gods. Maybe it is Christianity, which believes that there is a Trinitarian God.

Each person must answer this question, through further study, for themselves to determine which religion is actually true. But first, we need to establish that there are objective truths in religion.

I believe the Bible is the *absolute*, objective, truth. But don't take my word for it. Study and discover for yourself and encourage your kids to do the same.

God gave us His Word, so we would know the truth and would not be deceived. Without the existence of objective truth, the Christian faith has no power. Truth is foundational to our faith.

"Two-thirds of Americans now deny there's any such thing as truth."[143]
—Lee Strobel, *The Case For Faith*

Our kids must leave our homes with the keen ability to identify and defend truth. Establishing that truth is not relative or subjective, but rather, objective and absolute, is essential to our kids' faith.

2. How Do I Know God Exists?

The most fundamental question of apologetics is *does God exist?* And, if God does exist, *what kind of god is He?*

There are two ways that God reveals Himself. God reveals Himself through *General Revelation* and *Special Revelation.*

According to Dr. Erwin W. Lutzer, "Revelation is the free act of God by which He graciously condescends to display and reveal His character, nature, and will to mankind."[144]

In the previous chapter, we talked about the importance of having our kids read Scripture. The Word of God, the Bible, is *Special Revelation.* In order to know God we must read His Word.

We know the Bible teaches there is a God, and it reveals a good deal of His character. But for many people, that isn't enough. There is a common attitude among Christians that says "If the Bible says it, than I believe it, and that settles it." This just doesn't cut it. What good is teaching from the Bible, if whoever you're speaking with doesn't believe that the Bible is true? Something else is needed.

That something else is *General Revelation.* God has also revealed Himself in nature. If science is the pursuit of the truth of the natural world, than it will always point to God. *And* it will always agree with Scripture.

Do we need to learn both?

My brother, Greg, who is a missionary and has studied Christian apologetics for ten years, put it this way:

We need *both* forms of revelation to make the complete case for Christianity. Just as we would all agree that General Revelation without the Bible is insufficient, I would say that the Bible without General Revelation is insufficient as well...the Bible shouldn't be taught at the exclusion of God's revelation in nature.

We must not exclude the natural world, God's creation, when seeking to know Him. The more ways we can learn about God, the more our faith will grow. The more we see His imprint in the natural world, the more in awe of Him we will be.

Stunning sunsets, dazzling stars twinkling across the night sky, or the sound of a mighty river rushing down a mountain fill us with awe and wonder. And awe and wonder lead us to the foot of the cross in reverence and worship.

Familiarity with the topic of General Revelation will help our kids defend their faith if they are challenged.

Science and Religion

Did you know that science, *does not*, in fact, disprove the existence of God? Historically, the church has been threatened by science. But, it poses no threat. God created everything. He is the author of truth. If science is the quest for truth, it will always point to *Him*.

Science **does not** disprove the existence of God.

As Christians, science is our friend and ally. Especially when talking about reaching young people for Christ.

David Kinnaman observes in his book, *You Lost Me,* that young Christians feel as if they have to choose between faith and science.

Every week, I am contacted by young Christians who tell me that their faith cannot survive their interest in science. They feel the church has forced them into an either or decision—they can either stay true to the Christian faith or become an intellectually honest scientist...

Issues of science are one of the significant points of disconnection between the next generation and Christianity.[145]

Science is the pursuit of truth. Therefore, we do not have to choose between science and faith.

Science presents us with questions. It offers mystery and the opportunity for exploration. Compared to science, religion comes across as arrogant. While some Christians think they have all the answers *(they don't!)*, science is asking questions.

According to Tim Suttle of the Princeton Theological Seminary,

> The ability to hold competing answers in unresolved tension, the embrace of mystery and paradox, these are the marks of a mature faith. Certitude cannot drive the process if we want young people on board.[146]

Young people on college campuses and universities will more likely be challenged in their faith scientifically, which is an issue of General Revelation, rather than scripturally.

Arguments

Why are questions like, *Why do you believe in God* or *How do you know God exists?* so difficult to answer? Many of us answer these questions by saying, "I just do," or, "I just know." There is nothing wrong with these answers.

I experience God's power and presence. I feel His immense love, grace, and mercy. Everything in my being knows He's there. This is how I know God exists.

However, to those who don't believe in God, vague answers like "I just know," or answers about feelings, won't cut it.

Some people need to have solid reasons to believe in God. Some people will need evidence. All Christians, but especially the youth, need to be equipped with arguments based on scientific facts and evidence that point to God and the truth of Christianity.

On the forefront of Christian apologetics is Dr. William Lane Craig. Dr. Craig has participated in numerous debates with the question, *Does God exist?* And he often addresses this topic with the help of the Cosmological Argument, the Teleological Argument (fine tuning), and the Moral Argument.

The Cosmological Argument contends that whatever begins to exist has a cause. In other words, something can't come from nothing, therefore, the universe had a cause. And God was that cause. This answers the question *Why believe in God?*

Something cannot come from nothing

According to Dr. Craig, "Something cannot come from nothing. To claim that something can come into being from nothing is worse than magic. When a magician pulls a rabbit out of a hat, at least you've got the magician, not to mention the hat!"[147]

The Teleological Argument has to do with intelligent design. It basically states that the fine-tuning of the universe is due to either necessity, chance, or *design*.[148]

In a short video from Reasonable Faith, the ministry of Dr. Craig (reasonablefaith.org), compelling evidence is given that *design* is the explanation for the fine-tuning of the universe.

Scientists have come to the shocking realization that each of these numbers (the constants and quantities of the universe) have been carefully dialed to an astonishingly precise value—a value that falls within an exceedingly narrow, life-permitting range. If any one of these numbers were altered by even a hair's breadth, no physical, interactive life of any kind could exist anywhere. There'd be no stars, no life, no planets, no chemistry.[149]

To entertain the thought that our universe could begin spontaneously is absurd if you study this argument. A universe such as ours, with such intricate design, demands a Designer.

"The laws (of physics)...seem to be the product of exceedingly ingenious design."[150]
–Paul Davies, British astrophysicist

The Moral Argument seeks to answer the question, *Can you be good without God?* Could moral values exist without God?

My daughters have recently started driving. Teaching your kids to drive ranks right up there with potty training and explaining the birds and the bees! As I sat next to each one of them in the passenger seat, I instructed them.

- *You have to yield! You don't have the right of way.*
- *Slow down! You can't go over the speed limit.*
- *Always use your turn signal so other drivers know what you're doing.*

Are the rules of the road innate? Were we born knowing them? Of course not. The government makes the laws, and we are expected to follow them.

Why did we have to be home by eleven when we were teenagers? Why did we finish our homework before we played with friends? Because of a higher authority—*our parents.* Why do kids have to get a hall pass to go to the bathroom during class? Because of a higher authority—*the school.* Why do we have to take a class to become members at church? Because of a higher authority—*the church.* Why do we have to be at work by 8:30? Because of a higher authority—*the boss.* Why do we have to wait until we are twenty-one to drink alcohol, or until we are eighteen to vote? Because of a higher authority—*the government.*

We will always have to obey rules. And all rules come from a higher power.

Euthyphro Dilemma:
Does God will something because it is good,
or is something good because God wills it?

Goodness or moral values fall into the same category as rules, and therefore, must come from a higher authority.

Does God have to exist for moral values to exist? Well, yes! All of the rules that we follow come from a higher authority. And *He* is the highest.

Much like the universe, moral values and duties must have a cause. Everything comes from something. Nothing in the material universe can exist uncaused or uncreated, *except* God.

Exposing our kids to these common questions and arguments can strengthen their faith. The more evidence you have of something, the more confident you will be that it is true. Knowing arguments for the truth that God exists will equip our kids so they can be confident when their faith is challenged.

Check out these short, entertaining and informative videos with your kids on the Cosmological Argument, the Teleological Argument, and the Moral Argument. They are fascinating.

http://www.reasonablefaith.org/kalam
http://www.reasonablefaith.org/finetuning
http://www.reasonablefaith.org/moral

3. Why Do I Believe Jesus is the Son of God?

The one detail that separates Christianity from all other religions is Jesus Christ. No other religion offers us a savior who covers our sins. He is central. He is everything.

Sadly, in recent times, Jesus has been reduced to a prophet, a good teacher, or just a good man. However, He is nothing less than the Son of God.

Author, speaker, Christian apologist, and Founder and Chairman of the Board of Ravi Zacharias International Ministries, Ravi Zacharias, spoke of the historical truths of Jesus in Lee Strobel's book, *The Case For Faith.*

> No man spoke like Jesus. No one ever answered the questions the way He answered them…The Bible is not just a book of mysticism or spirituality; it is a book that also gives geographical truths and historical truths. If you're an honest skeptic, it's not just calling you to a feeling; it's calling you to a real person.[151]

Is there compelling evidence to the truth of Jesus' death and resurrection? Yes, there is. I recommend the following books: *A Case For Christ* by Lee Strobel; *New Evidence That Demands a Verdict* by Josh McDowell; or *I Don't Have Enough Faith to be an Atheist* by Norman L. Geisler and Frank Turek.

You may have heard of the Lunatic, Liar, Lord Argument for the divinity of Christ popularized by C.S. Lewis.

1. **Liar** - Jesus claimed to be the Son of God, but knew that He wasn't.
2. **Lunatic** - Jesus claimed to be the Son of God, and He didn't know that He wasn't.
3. **Lord** - Jesus claimed to be the Son of God and He was.

According to Watchman Nee in his 1936 book, *Normal Christian Faith,* deductive reasoning leads to a logical conclusion.

> There is no need for us to prove if Jesus of Nazareth is God or not. All we have to do is find out if He is a lunatic or a liar. If He is neither, He must be the Son of God.[152]

One must bend over backwards to refute the truth of the resurrection. The evidence that Jesus did rise from the dead is overwhelming. Therefore, with all of the evidence pointing to the truth of Jesus' claims that He was the Son of

God, I submit to Ockham's Razor, which states that the simplest explanation tends to be the right one.

4. Why Do I Believe the Bible Is True?

The Bible is the most widely circulated book in the world. It has survived throughout the ages despite immense opposition. It is also our source of hope and peace. Scripture contains words of life and freedom. It is sacred and precious. It is the foundation of our faith. *But is it true? Is it reliable?*

Many have called the Bible, "a good book," or "a book of stories and fables." What would our kids say about the Bible? Do they know without a doubt that Scripture is the true and definitive Word of God?

Is there compelling evidence that the Bible is the true Word of God? Yes, there is. Ravi Zacharias in Josh McDowell's *New Evidence That Demands A Verdict*, talks about the integrity of the New Testament.

The New Testament is easily the best attested ancient writing in terms of the sheer number of documents, the time span between the events and the document, and the variety of documents available to sustain or contradict it. There is nothing in ancient manuscript evidence to match such textual availability and integrity.[153]

Author and president at Southern Evangelical Seminary in Charlotte, North Carolina, Norman Geisler addresses the prophesies in the Bible.

The Bible is the only book in the world that has precise, specific predictions that were made hundreds of years in advance and that were literally fulfilled.[154]

Dr. Gleason Archer was a biblical scholar, theologian, educator, and author. He had this to say about the contradictions in the Bible.

There is a good and sufficient answer in Scripture itself to refute every charge that has ever been leveled against it.[155]

Sir William Ramsay, regarded as one of the greatest archaeologist, had great confidence in the gospel of Luke.

> Luke is a historian of the first rank; not merely are his statements of fact trustworthy…this author should be placed along with the very greatest of historians…Luke's history is unsurpassed in respect of its trustworthiness.[156]

5. How Does Being a Christian Affect My Life?

Most kids who grow up in the church are not living out their faith. You see it. I see it. They are not connecting the dots.

According to Josh McDowell in his book, *The Last Christian Generation,* "research showed that ninety-eight percent of professed born-again young people do believe in Christ, but they do not reflect Christ-like attitudes or actions."[157]

In order to understand why this is so, we must understand the concept of *worldviews.*

Nancy Fitzgerald, author and founder of Anchorsaway ministries, explains that "a worldview is the foundation from which one lives, views life, thinks and responds to the world in which he/she lives."[158]

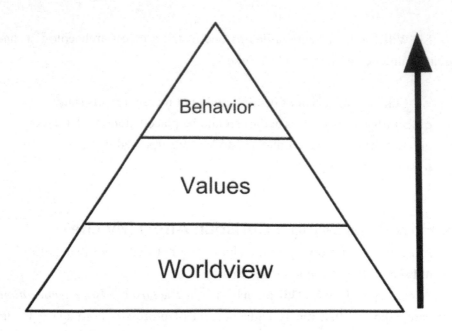

This illustration connects the dots between our kids' lifestyles and their worldviews. Worldviews yield our kids' values and in turn values are expressed in behaviors.

Fitzgerald goes on the say, "Our behavior is shaped by our values, which are ultimately built upon the foundation of our worldview."[159]

Our kids' behavior and lifestyles are not shaped by their religion, they are shaped by their *worldview*. Their religion might be Christianity, but if they have not decided to live out a Biblical worldview, then they are not likely to act out their faith.

Our kids' behavior and lifestyles are not shaped by their religion, they are shaped by their **worldview**.

There are many worldviews across the globe today. From religious extremists who kill innocent people in the name of Allah, to young Americans who have thrown away truth in the quest to create their own reality. Differing worldviews abound.

According to Dennis McCallum, there are five major worldviews: Theism, Naturalism, Pantheism, Spiritism, and Postmodernism.[160]

Theism holds that there is one God and He acts on our behalf. Christianity is a theistic worldview, which consists of one third of the world's population.[161] Judaism and Islam also have a theistic worldview.

Those who practice *Naturalism,* according to *The Stanford Encyclopedia of Philosophy*, believe "the scientific method should be used to investigate all areas of reality, including the human spirit."[162] Believers in Naturalism deny the existence of the supernatural. This would include atheism, agnosticism, and existentialism.

Phillip E. Johnson in his book, *Darwin on Trial*, connects science with naturalism.

Theistic or "guided" evolution has to be excluded as a possibility because Darwinists identify science with a philosophical doctrine known as naturalism. Naturalism assumes the entire realm of nature to be a closed system of material causes and effects, which cannot be influenced by anything from "outside."[163]

Naturalists believe that science holds all the answers to understanding life, to mankind's full potential, and is the key to progress, individual freedom, human reason, self-determination, and tolerance.[164] It comes back to man being at the center and God being unnecessary.

Google defines *Pantheism* as "a doctrine that identifies God with the universe, or regards the universe as a manifestation of God." This worldview believes everything is interconnected, God is in everything, and the universe is divine. Hinduism, Taoism, Buddhism, and New Age are Pantheistic worldviews.[165]

Spiritism consists of thousands of religions around the world. The main emphasis of this worldview is on contact with spirits. According to the Toronto Spiritist Society, followers of Spiritism believe "death is not the end of life and man continues to live as a spirit being who can communicate with those living in this world." The use of shamans, or mediums, would fall into this worldview.

The most prevalent worldview in our country today is Postmodernism.

Postmodernism is also called, deconstructionism[166] because its believers tend to deconstruct established truths. They are skeptical and suspicious. They don't believe in God. They don't believe in truth. And they don't believe in absolute morality. People with this worldview look for quick fixes because their focus is on feelings. And they prefer the *experiential* to the rational.[167]

Postmodernism is a hopeless worldview. There is no God. There is no meaning. There is no foundation with which to build. And when you die, that's it.

This worldview can be seen in the passive attitudes of many young people today. Recognizing Postmodernism can help us explain the presence of dysfunctional elements in our culture.

> *"Students are continually told in today's culture that the Bible is unreliable, that Jesus was no different than any other religious figure, and that anyone who asserts there is an objective truth that shapes a worldview is intolerant and a bigot…If ever there was a time to make a concerted effort to instill a biblical worldview into the next generation—a way to think from a biblical perspective—it's now."[168]*
> —Josh McDowell and Sean McDowell, *The Unshakable Truth*

Moralistic Therapeutic Deism…*oh my!*

As we talked about previously, truth is foundational to our faith. And everyone has a belief system, even if they don't call it "religion." Young people often fuse together various aspects of religion and personal desires to form their own belief system.

Kenda Creasy Dean quotes Christian Smith and Melinda Denton in her book, *Almost Christian*, as saying that American teenagers have found an "alternative faith that feeds on and gradually co-opts if not devours"[169] religions.

She goes on to introduce the guiding beliefs of *Moralistic Therapeutic Deism*.

Moralistic Therapeutic Deism (MTD)

1. A god exists who created and orders the world and watches over life on earth.
2. God wants people to be good, nice, and fair to each other.
3. The central goal of life is to be happy and to feel good about oneself.
4. God is not involved in my life except when I need God to resolve a problem.
5. Good people go to heaven when they die.[170]

MTD describes the passive faith I had in college and into my twenties. Although I claimed to be a Christian, I did not adopt a Biblical worldview. And I didn't connect my faith to my lifestyle.

If we don't emphasize the importance of living a *Biblical* worldview, our kids are likely to adopt this belief system when they go out in the world. They may never notice the inconsistency between their life and faith.

———

I have not even begun to scratch the surface on the topic of apologetics. My goal is to introduce it and give an overview. And maybe to whet your appetite. What I have included in this chapter is nowhere near enough information to equip you or your kids.

I beg you. Dig deeper. Ask questions. Learn more.

Without knowledge of apologetics and worldviews, we are sending our kids into battle with no protection and no gear. Without the proper gear, they will likely wave the white flag at their colleges and universities and give up their faith.

Questions you need to think through with your child include:

- *Is the God of the Bible the same or different than other gods?*
- *How is Christianity different than other religions?*
- *What are common arguments against Christianity?*
- *How do we best answer those arguments?*

We must take the time to get answers to these questions and the others I have posed in this chapter.

Anchorsaway is a great resource. This ministry is built around a curriculum that teaches high school juniors and seniors about apologetics and worldviews. "Anchorsaway students will learn how to build an authentic faith in Christ and will be prepared to give an answer to others as to what they believe to be true about God, Jesus Christ, and the Bible."[171]

Check out their website, anchorsaway.org, for more information or to find a class near you.

In the area of apologetics, I suggest the books, *I Don't Have Enough Faith to be an Atheist,* by Norman Geisler and Frank Turek, *A Case for Christ,* or *A Case for Faith* by Lee Strobel, or *The New Evidence That Demands a Verdict* by Josh McDowell.

For additional resources, visit my Resources page at
www.livingtolovehim.com

Conclusion

As I write this, both my girls are in Tegucigalpa, Honduras, on a mission trip. I am so proud of them. My husband and I have been praying for God to work in their hearts during this time. We pray that God would break their hearts for what breaks His.

They're gone, in another country, without me. The house is quiet, and the days are long. I miss them terribly. And it doesn't help that my husband keeps reminding me that in three short years, the girls will be gone.

My husband and I are approaching the *empty nest* at which point, I will have been a stay-at-home mom for twenty years. *Twenty years!* I hardly remember who I was before we built the nest.

I love being a mom. It's been the joy of my life. While I will always be their mom, it won't be like it is now. I'm getting a taste of life without them. And I don't like it. Not that I have a choice in the matter.

There are seasons, I know. It's just more comfortable being in the middle of one, than at the end. It's hard to say goodbye.

My girls don't belong to my husband and I, however, they belong to God. We only get them for a time—a precious season.

While loving our kids well is number one, our job as parents involves many things. We need to show them what it looks like to follow Christ. We must raise our kids to *know* their Creator and Savior. Not just to know *of* Him.

> *These commandments that I give you today are to be on your hearts.*
> *Impress them on your children. Talk about them when you sit at home*
> *and when you walk along the road, when you lie down, and when you get*
> *up. Tie them as symbols on your hands and bind them on your foreheads.*
> *Write them on the doorframes of your houses and on your gates.*
> Deuteronomy 6:5-9

We desire for our sons and daughters to grow up to be Godly men and women. We strive to foster the growth of holiness in them. By modeling Christ, we attempt to raise up human beings with the capacity for extreme love and humility. Our aim is to raise followers of Christ who are compassionate, merciful, and full of grace.

Our job is to raise people who love well, live for eternity, and resemble Christ. We want our kids to be selfless people who have a servant's heart. And we must teach our kids that they must be different if they are going to follow Christ.

The bottom line is we must teach our kids to put Christ above everything, and in turn, do what He says in Scripture.

Flush the Formula

However, even if we do everything right, there is no guarantee our kids will continue to follow Christ when they leave our homes.

A plus B does not always equal C—no matter how desperately we want it to. There is no formula for this life. We must follow God's leading and trust Him with our kids every day.

The faith of our kids is ultimately out of our hands. At some point, we must release our kids into *His* loving and able hands.

The battle is not ours. And praise God for it! Because we don't have what it takes.

This is what the Lord says to you: "Do not be afraid or discouraged because of this vast army. For the battle is not yours, but God's."
2 Chronicles 20:15

We are soldiers, we are not the commander. We must follow orders from above and stand firm.

I see my everyday failures as an opportunity to be reminded of how inadequate, and *not God* I am. I am thankful that we are not in control. Because if we were, we would thoroughly screw things up.

I want my daughters to feel free to fail, to feel free not to have the answers, to feel free to be human. There is rest and comfort in that.

And now that they are young women, I want them to think of God as their safe place to fall. I want them to know He completely loves and accepts them as they are. They are His *beloved*.

We have been given an invitation to the royal ball when there is seemingly nothing *royal* about us. We are Cinderella. We are messy and unworthy to gain the attention, love, and acceptance of the prince. Yet, in spite of it all, the prince has fallen madly in love with us.

How awesome is our God!

Prayer

The most powerful thing that we can do for our kids, however, is to go to God and beg Him for His favor. Prayer is powerful.

Therefore confess your sins to each other and pray for each other so that you may be healed. The prayer of a righteous person is powerful and effective.
James 5:16

We must pray for our kids. God listens when we seek His voice and pray for right things.

We must never cease to pray as we raise our kids. Pray that God would draw our kids' heart to His. Pray for their calling to be revealed. Pray for their future spouses. Pray for their friends. Pray that they would put God first in their lives. And pray that we, as their parents, would represent Christ well.

Someone once said to me, if you were a perfect parent, your kids wouldn't need a Savior. Amen! They were so right.

Most of our kids would say that they love Jesus. However, we need to be in constant prayer that our kids would fall in love with Jesus. Pray that their love and devotion for Him would invade every cell of their body. Pray that they can't stand to be separated from him. Pray our kids would not only believe *in* God, but *believe* Him. And pray they would move from just loving God, to completely surrendering to Him.

The Mission

Raising teenagers is tougher than I ever imagined. The hearts of my teenage girls are fragile and tender. And teaching them to follow Jesus and obey the Word of God in this world seems like an impossible task.

The more I talk with my kids, the more I realize that between school, all their devices, texting, and social media, they are living in a toxic world.

We can't change the entire world, but we can change our kids' worlds to show them more of Christ.

Let's commit to raising Kingdom-focused families who are eternity-focused, rather than American Dream-focused.

Let's put on humility instead of pride. Let's become God-focused instead of self-focused. Let's define success according to God's Word and not American culture. And let's teach the next generation to depend on God, not themselves.

It's all about *Him*.

"Good parenting means showing your children that the mission is bigger
than any of us."[72]
—Francis and Lisa Chan, *You and Me, Forever*

Let our mission as Christian families be to love and know God more and spread the gospel to the ends of the earth. The mission is bigger than our kids or our families.

> *Then Jesus came to them and said, "All authority in heaven and on earth has been given to me. Therefore go and make disciples of all nations, baptizing them in the name of the Father and of the Son and of the Holy Spirit, and teaching them to obey everything I have commanded you. And surely I am with you always, to the very end of the age."*
> Matthew 28:18-20

About the Author

Kim Kurtz is a new writer in the trenches of raising two delightful and challenging teenagers. Originally from Farmington Hills, Michigan, Kim now lives in Westfield, Indiana, with her husband Jamie and two daughters Emily and Jessica. She believes that words are powerful and precious.

For more information about Kim and to check out her blog, please visit: www.livingtolovehim.com. Check out Kim on Facebook, @KimKurtzauthor, and Twitter, @KimeKurtz.

Notes

Introduction: Tipping the Scales in Favor of Faith

1   Josh McDowell, *The Last Christian Generation* (Holiday, FL: Green Key Books, 2006), 13.

2   Dr. Kara E. Powell and Dr. Chap Clark, *Sticky Faith: Everyday Ideas to Build Lasting Faith in Your Kids* (Grand Rapids, MI: Zondervan, 2011), 23-24.

3   Beth Moore, *Entrusted: A Study of 2 Timothy* (Nashville: Lifeway Press, 2016), 148.

4   gotQuestions?org, "Why are So Many Young People Falling Away from the Faith?" https://www.gotquestions.org/falling-away.html.

5   David Kinnaman, *You Lost Me. Why Young Christians are Leaving Church... And Rethinking Faith* (Grand Rapids, MI: BakerBooks, 2011), 232.

Chapter 1: My Story, A Tale of Four Cousins

6   Hayden Shaw, *Generational IQ* (Carol Stream, IL: Tyndale House Publishers, 2015), 13.

7   Ibid, 17.

8   Beth Moore, *Children of the Day: 1 and 2 Thessalonians* (Nashville: LifeWay Press, 2014). 60-61.

9   Kara Powell, Jake Mulder, and Brad Griffin, *Growing Young: Six Essential Strategies to Help Young People Discover and Love Your Church* (Grand Rapids, MI: BakerBooks, 2016), 58.

10   Steve Argue quoted by Brad M. Griffin, "Three Words Every Young Person Wants to Hear," *Fuller Youth Institute* (blog), March 17, 2017, https:// fulleryouthinstitute.org/blog/three-words.

11   David Kinnaman and Gabe Lyons, *Good Faith: Being a Christian When Society Thinks You're Irrelevant and Extreme* (Grand Rapids, MI: BakerBooks, 2016), 126.

Chapter 2: Houston, We Have a Problem

12   Hayden Shaw, *Generational IQ* (Carol Stream, IL: Tyndale House Publishers, 2015), 176-177.

13   "Cosmos: A Personal Voyage," *Wikipedia*, last modified July 23, 2017, https://en.wikipedia.org/wiki/Cosmos:_A_Personal_Voyage.

14   Miss Cellania, "Forty Years Ago: Apollo 13," *Mental Floss* (blog), April 13, 2010, http://mentalfloss.com/article/24441/forty-years-ago-apollo-13.

15   Maggie Galehouse, "Forty Years after Apollo 13, Five Words Remain Linked to City," *Chron*, April 12, 2010, http://www.chron.com/news/houston-texas/article/40-years-after-Apollo-13-five-words-remain-1694332.php.

16   Josh McDowell, *The Last Christian Generation* (Holiday, FL: Green Key Books, 2006), 11.

17   Frank Turek, quoted by Lysa Terkeurst, "Before Sending My Child to College," (blog), May 19, 2008, http://lysaterkeurst.com/2008/05/before-sending-my-child-to-college/.

18   Josh McDowell and Sean McDowell, *The Unshakable Truth, How You Can Experience the Twelve Essentials of a Relevant Faith* (Eugene, OR: Harvest House Publishers, 2010), 21.

19   Brent Kunkle, "Intellectual Skepticism in Our Youth," *Stand to Reason*, (blog), March 29, 2011, https://www.str.org/blog/intellectual-skepticism-in-our-youth#.WV5X6ITyvX5.

20   Ken Ham and Britt Beemer, *Already Gone: Why Your Kids Will Quit Church and What You Can Do to Stop it* (Green Forest, AR: Master Books, 2009), 23.

21   Ibid, 19.

22   Ibid, 31.

23   Dr. Kara Powell and Dr. Chap Clark, *Sticky Faith: Everyday Ideas to Build Lasting Faith in Your Kids* (Grand Rapids, MI: Zondervan, 2011), 26.

24   Ibid, 16.

25   David Kinnaman, *You Lost Me. Why Young Christians are Leaving Church... and Rethinking Faith* (Grand Rapids, MI: BakerBooks, 2011), 115.

26   Josh McDowell, *The Last Christian Generation* (Holiday, FL: Greek Key Books, 2006), 14.

27   Ibid, 15.

28   Kara Powell, Jake Mulder, and Brad Griffin, *Growing Young: Six Essential Strategies to Help Young People Discover and Love Your Church* (Grand Rapids, MI: Baker Books, September, 2016), 14.

29   Ibid, 16.

30   Dr. Kara Powell and Dr. Chap Clark, *Sticky Faith: Everyday Ideas to Build Lasting Faith in Your Kids* (Grand Rapids, MI: Zondervan, September, 2011), 17.

31   Ibid, 18.

32   Dr. Michael Kimmel quoted by Dr. Kara Powell and Dr. Chap Clark, *Sticky Faith: Everyday Ideas to Build Lasting Faith in Your Kids* (Grand Rapids, MI: Zondervan, September, 2011), 18.

33   Frank Turek, quoted by Lysa Terkeurst, "Before Sending My Child to College," (blog), May 19, 2008, http://lysaterkeurst.com/2008/05/before-sending-my-child-to-college/.

34   Rose Eveleth, "There are 37.2 Trillion Cells in Your Body," *Smithsonian.com*, October 24, 2013, http://www.smithsonianmag.com/smart-news/there-are-372-trillion-cells-in-your-body-4941473/.

Chapter 3: Why are Our Kids Leaving the Church? Digging in the Soil

35   David Kinnaman, *You Lost Me. Why Young Christians are Leaving Church... and Rethinking Faith* (Grand Rapids, MI: Baker Books, 2011), 202.

36   Matt Bays, *Finding God in the Ruins* (Colorado Springs, CO: David C Cook, 2016), 112.

37   Josh McDowell, *The Last Christian Generation* (Holiday, FL: Green Key Books, 2006), 19-20.

Chapter 4: Why are Our Kids Leaving the Church? Contributing Factors

38   Charlie Peacock quoted by David Kinnaman, *You Lost Me. Why Young Christians are Leaving Church...and Rethinking Faith* (Grand Rapids, MI: BakerBooks, 2011), 217.

39   Francis Chan quoted by David Kinnaman, *You Lost Me. Why Young Christians are Leaving Church...and Rethinking Faith* (Grand Rapids, MI: Baker Books, 2011), 216.

40   David Kinnaman, *You Lost Me. Why Young Christians are Leaving Church... and Rethinking Faith* (Grand Rapids, MI: Baker Books, 2011), 27.

41   Frank Turek, "The Seeker Church: Is Anyone Making Disciples?" *CrossExamined.org* (blog), December 20, 2007, http://crossexamined.org/the-seeker-church-protestant-roman-catholicism/.

42   Josh McDowell and Sean McDowell, *The Unshakable Truth, How You Can Experience the Twelve Essentials of a Relevant Faith* (Eugene, OR: Harvest House Publishers, 2010), 24.

43   Sam Williamson, "Why Do Our Kids Reject Christianity?" *The Noble Heart* (blog), March 29, 2016, http://thenobleheart.com/2016/03/why-do-our-kids-reject-christianity/.

44   Kara Powell, *Growing Young, Six Strategies to Help Young People Discover and Love Your Church* (Grand Rapids, MI: Baker Books, 2016), 150-151.

45   "Thirty-two Shocking Divorce Statistics," *McKinley Irvin Law Firm,* October 30, 2012, https://www.mckinleyirvin.com/Family-Law-Blog/2012/October/32-Shocking-Divorce-Statistics.aspx.

46   Joe Carter, "Twenty-five Facts on the Importance of Fathers," *The Gospel Coalition* (blog), June 13, 2014, //www.thegospelcoalition.org/article/25-facts-on-the-importance-of-fathers.

47   "The Extent of Fatherlessness," *National Center for Fathering,* http://www.fathers.com/statistics-and-research/the-extent-of-fatherlessness/.

48   Ibid.

Chapter 5: Are We Different?

49   Kenda Creasy Dean, *Almost Christian: What the Faith of Our Teenagers is Telling the American Church* (New York: Oxford University Press, 2010), 25.

50   David Kinnaman and Gabe Lyons, *Good Faith: Being a Christian When Society Thinks You're Being Irrelevant and Extreme* (Grand Rapids, MI: Baker Books, 2016), 260.

51   Dallas Willard, *The Great Omission* (New York: HarperCollins, 2006), 3.

52   Ibid, x.

53   David Kinnaman and Gabe Lyons, *Good Faith, Being a Christian When Society Thinks You're Being Irrelevant and Extreme* (Grand Rapids, MI: Baker Books, 2016), 224.

54   Ibid, 27.

55   Ibid, 224.

56   Ibid, 27.

57   Ibid, 51.

58   Kimberly Amadeo, "Halloween Spending Statistics, Facts and Trends," *The Balance* (blog), October 6, 2016, https://www.thebalance.com/halloween-spending-statistics-facts-and-trends-3305716.

59   Jim Kinney, "How Much Will Americans Spend on Christmas 2016?" *Mass Live* (blog), November 16, 2016, http://www.masslive.com/business-news/index.ssf/2016/11/christmas_2016_how_much_will_americans_s.html.

60   Bryan Pearson, "Holiday Spending To Exceed One Trillion Dollars and Eleven Other Surprising Data Points of Christmas," *Forbes,* December 22, 2016, https://www.forbes.com/sites/bryanpearson/2016/12/22/holiday-spending-to-exceed-1-trillion-and-11-other-surprising-data-points-of-christmas/#fb41327247fe.

61   Tami Luhby, "Seventy-one Percent of the World's Population Lives on Less Than Ten Dollars a Day," *CNN,* July 8, 2015, http://money.cnn.com/2015/07/08/news/economy/global-low-income/.

62   "Eleven Facts about Global Poverty," *DOsomething.org,* https://www.dosomething.org/us/facts/11-facts-about-global-poverty.

63   David Kinnaman and Gabe Lyons, *Good Faith: Being a Christian When Society Thinks You're Irrelevant and Extreme* (Grand Rapids, MI: Baker Books, 2016), 261-262.

Chapter 6: Three Elements of a Contagious Faith: First, Love

64   David Kinnaman, *You Lost Me. Why Young Christians are Leaving Church...* *and Rethinking Faith* (Grand Rapids, MI: Baker Books, 2011), 209.

65   Francis Chan, *Crazy Love* (Colorado Springs: David C Cook, 2013) 103-104.

66   Dr. Georgia Purdom, "Laminin and the Cross," *Answers in Genesis,* October 29, 2008, https://answersingenesis.org/biology/microbiology/laminin-and-the-cross/.

67   Gary Chapman, *The Five Love Languages* (Chicago, IL: Northfield Publishing, 2015).

68   Beth Moore, *Audacious,* (Nashville: B&H Publishing Group, 2015), 28.

69   Francis Chan, *Crazy Love,* (Colorado Springs: David C Cook, 2013) 96-97.

Chapter 7: Three Elements of a Contagious Faith: Second, Humility

70   C.S. Lewis, *Mere Christianity* (New York: HarperCollins Publishers, 1980), 127.

71   Ibid, 121-122.

72   Beth Moore, *Believing God* (Nashville: Lifeway Press, 2004), 191.

73   Michael Reeves, *Rejoicing in Christ* (Downers Grove, IL: InterVarsity Press, 2015), 62.

74   Beth Moore, *Believing God* (Nashville, TN: Lifeway Press, 2004), 191.

75   C.S. Lewis, *Mere Christianity* (New York: HarperCollins Publishers, 1980), 125.

76   Billy Hallowell, "Christian Grammy Winner Reveals Why She Purposefully Decided Not to Attend the Award Show," *The Blaze,* Jan 28, 2014, http://www.theblaze.com/stories/2014/01/28/christian-grammy-winner-reveals-why-she-purposefully-decided-not-to-attend/.

77   Ibid.

78   C.S. Lewis, *Mere Christianity* (New York: HarperCollins Publishers, 1980), 128.

79   Paul Gould, "The Vice of Self-Confidence," (blog), http://www.paul-gould.com/2015/10/07/the-vice-of-self-confidence/.

80 Ibid.

Chapter 8: Three Elements of a Contagious Faith: Third, Surrender

81 Francis Chan and Lisa Chan, *You and Me Forever: Marriage in Light of Eternity* (San Francisco: Claire Love Publishing, 2014), 161.

82 Pat Conroy, "Interpreting the World through Story," *The Writer* (blog), March 9, 2016, https://www.writermag.com/2016/03/09/pat-conroy/.

83 Dr. Henry Cloud and Dr. John Townsend, *Twelve "Christian" Beliefs That Can Drive You Crazy* (Grand Rapids, MI: Zondervan, 1995) 16.

84 Dr. Kara Powell and Dr. Chap Clark, *Sticky Faith, Everyday Ideas to Build Lasting Faith in Your Kids* (Grand Rapids, MI: Zondervan, 2011), 46.

85 "Earthquake in Haiti" *International Rescue Committee*, January 12, 2015, https://www.rescue.org/article/earthquake-haiti.

86 Ivan Watson, Jethro Mullen, and Laura Smith-Spark, "Nepal Earthquake: Death Toll Passes forty-eight hundred as Rescuers Face Challenges," *CNN*, April 28, 2015, http: //www.cnn.com/2015/04/28/asia/nepal-earthquake/index.html.

87 "The Deadliest Tsunami in History?" *National Geographic*, last modified January 7, 2005 http://news.nationalgeographic.com/news/2004/12/1227_041226_tsunami.html.

88 "Columbine High School Massacre," *Wikipedia*, last modified July 28, 2017, https://en.wikipedia.org/wiki/Columbine_High_School_massacre.

89 Steve Vogel, Sari Horwitz, and David A. Fahrenthold, " Sandy Hook Elementary Shooting Leaves Twenty-eight Dead, Law Enforcement Sources Say," *The Washington Post*, December 14, 2012, https://www.washingtonpost.com/politics/sandy-hook-elementary-school-shooting-leaves-students-staff-dead/2012/12/14/24334570-461e-11e2-8e70-e1993528222d_story.html.

90 "Nice Attack: What We Know about the Bastille Day Killings," *BBC News*, August 19, 2016, http://www.bbc.com/news/world-europe-36801671.

91 "1993 World Trade Center Bombing Fast Facts," *CNN*, last modified February 21, 2017, http://www.cnn.com/2013/11/05/us/1993-world-trade-center-bombing-fast-facts/.

92 "Oklahoma City Bombing," *History*, http://www.history.com/topics/oklahoma-city-bombing.

93 Diana Lynne, "Littlest Victims Largely Overlooked," *World Net Daily*, December 21,2001, http://www.wnd.com/2001/12/12105/.

94 Reggie Joiner, *Parenting Beyond Your Capacity* (Colorado Springs: David C Cook, 2010), 180.

Chapter 9: Oh, to be Like You

95 "2643. Katallagé: Strong's Concordance," *Bible Hub*, http://biblehub.com/greek/2643.htm.

96 "Reconciliation-Katallage (Greek Word Study)," *Precept Austin*, last modified September 28, 2016, http://www.preceptaustin.org/reconciliation-katallage-greek-word-study.

97 Jon Nielson, 2017, "Three Common Traits of Youth Who Don't Leave the Church," *Church Leaders*, January 3, 2017, http://churchleaders.com/youth/youth-leaders-articles/159175-3-common-traits-of-youth-who-don-t-leave-the-church.html.

98 John Piper, *Desiring God*, (Colorado Springs: Multnomah Books, 1986), 64.

99 Ibid, 67.

100 "Sanctification," *Bible Study Tools*, http://www.biblestudytools.com/dictionary/sanctification/.

101 Dallas Willard, *The Great Omission* (New York: HarperCollins, 2006), 26.

102 Joyce Burlingame, *Living with Death, Dying with Life: The Story of an Incredible Journey* (Bloomington, IN: Westbow Press, 2015), July 9.

103 Adam S. McHugh, *Introverts in the Church: Finding Our Place in an Extroverted Culture* (Downers Grove, IL: IVP Books), 25.

Chapter 10: Truth, Reality, and the American Dream

104 "The Great Depression," *History,* http://www.history.com/topics/great-depression.

105 "American Dream," *Wikipedia*, last modified July 13, 2017, https://en.wikipedia.org/wiki/American_Dream.

106 Tom Sine, quoted by Walt Mueller, *Youth Culture 101* (Grand Rapids, MI: Zondervan, 2007), 69.

107 David Kinnaman and Gabe Lyons, *Good Faith: Being a Christian When Society Thinks You're Being Irrelevant and Extreme* (Grand Rapids, MI: Baker Books, 2016), 251.

108 Hayden Shaw, Generational IQ (Carol Stream, IL: Tyndale House Publishers), 46.

109 David Kinnaman and Gabe Lyons, *Good Faith: Being a Christian When Society Thinks You're Being Irrelevant and Extreme* (Grand Rapids, MI: Baker Books, 2016), 190.

110 David Batty, "Steve Jobs: From Parents' Garage to World Power," *The Guardian*, October 5, 2011, https://www.theguardian.com/technology/2011/oct/06/steve-jobs-timeline-apple.

111 Beth Moore, *Children of the Day: 1 and 2 Thessalonians* (Nashville: Lifeway Press, 2014), 121.

Chapter 11: The Power of *No*

112 Hayden Shaw, *Generational IQ* (Carol Stream, IL: Tyndale House Publishers, 2015), 123.

113 David Kinnaman and Gabe Lyons, *Good Faith: Being a Christian When Society Thinks You're Being Irrelevant and Extreme* (Grand Rapids, MI: Baker Books, 2016), 194.

114 Dr. Kara E. Powell and Dr. Chap Clark, *Sticky Faith: Everyday Ideas to Build Lasting Faith in Your Kids* (Grand Rapids, MI: Zondervan, 2011), 62.

115 Priscilla Shirer, *The Armor of God,* (Nashville: Lifeway Press, 2015), 93.

116 Hayden Shaw, *Generational IQ* (Carol Stream, IL: Tyndale House Publishers, 2015), 27.

117 Ibid, 34.

Chapter 12: Eleven False Mantras of Christian Parenting

118 Francis Chan and Lisa Chan, *You and Me Forever: Marriage in Light of Eternity* (San Francisco: Claire Love Publishing, 2014), 117.

119 David Kinnaman and Gabe Lyons, *Good Faith: Being a Christian When Society Thinks You're Being Irrelevant and Extreme* (Grand Rapids, MI: Baker Books, 2016), 133.

120 Tim Elmore, *Generation iY: Our Last Chance to Save Their Future* (Atlanta, GA: Poet Gardener Publishing, 2010), 20.

121 "Even If You Win the Rat Race, You're Still a Rat," *Quote Investigator*, http://quoteinvestigator.com/2014/09/28/rat-race/.

122 Richard A. Swenson, M.D., *Margin: Restoring Emotional, Physical, Financial, and Times Reserves to Overloaded Lives* (Colorado Springs: NavPress, 1992), 55.

123 Aaron Blake, "Mike Pence Doesn't Dine Alone with other Women and We're All Shocked," *The Washington Post*, March 30, 2017, https://www.washingtonpost.com/news/the-fix/wp/2017/03/30/mike-pence-doesnt-dine-alone-with-other-women-and-were-all-shocked/.

124 Oswald Chambers, *My Utmost for His Highest* (Grand Rapids, MI: Discovery House Publishers, 2012), Aug. 4.

125 Francis Chan and Lisa Chan, *You and Me Forever: Marriage in Light of Eternity* (San Francisco: Claire Love Publishing, 2014), 66.

Chapter 13: Actionable Intelligence

126 Gregory Elder, "Intelligence in War: It Can Be Decisive, Winning with Intelligence" *Central Intelligence Agency* Apr 15, 2007, https://www.cia.gov/library/center-for-the-study-of-intelligence/csi-publications/csi-studies/studies/vol50no2/html_files/Intelligence_War_2.htm.

127 "Definition of 'Actionable Intelligence'," *Collins*, https://www.collinsdictionary.com/us/dictionary/english/actionable-intelligence.

128 "Why are So Many Young People Falling Away from the Faith?" gotQuestions?org, https://www.gotquestions.org/falling-away.html.

129 David Kinnaman, *You Lost Me. Why Young Christians are Leaving Church... and Rethinking Faith* (Grand Rapids, MI: BakerBooks, 2011), 182.

130 Ibid, 52.

131 JD Greear, *Gospel, the Power That Made Christianity Revolutionary* (Nashville: B&H Publishing Group, 2011), 5.

132 Beth Moore, *Believing God* (Nashville: LifeWay Press, 2004), 124.

133 David Kinnaman, *You Lost Me. Why Young Christians are Leaving Church...* *and Rethinking Faith* (Grand Rapids, MI: BakerBooks, 2011), 197.

134 Beth Moore, *Believing God* (Nashville, TN: LIfeWay Press, 2004), 87.

135 John Ortberg and Jim Candy (foreword), Dr. Kara Powell and Dr. Chap Clark, *Sticky Faith: Everyday Ideas to Build Lasting Faith in Your Kids* (Grand Rapids, MI: Zondervan, 2011), 9-10.

136 "The Purpose Driven Life," *Wikipedia*, last modified February 20, 2017, https://en.wikipedia.org/wiki/The_Purpose_Driven_Life.

Chapter 14: Apologetics and Worldviews

137 Nancy Fitzgerald, *Anchorsaway Small Group Leader's Worldview Handbook*, (Carmel, IN: Anchorsaway, 2006), 1.

138 David Kinnaman, *You Lost Me. Why Young Christians are Leaving Church...* *and Rethinking Faith* (Grand Rapids, MI: BakerBooks, 2011), 12.

139 Daniel G. Thompson, "Behind the Veil of Mormon Temples," *AncestryWorship.com*, June 29, 2015, http://www.ancestryworship.com/ AncestryWorship/LDS_TOPICS/Entries/2015/6/29_BEHIND_THE_VEIL_OF_ MORMON_TEMPLES.html.

140 "List of Religions and Spiritual Traditions," *Wikipedia*, last modified July 26, 2017, https://en.wikipedia.org/wiki/List_of_religions_and_spiritual_traditions.

141 "627. Apologia: Strong's Concordance," *Bible Hub*, http:// http://biblehub. com/greek/627.htm.

142 Frank Turek and Norman L. Geisler, *I Don't Have Enough Faith to be an Atheist* (Wheaton, IL: Crossway, 2004), 8.

143 Lee Strobel, *The Case for Faith* (Grand Rapids, MI: Zondervan, 2000), 146.

144 Dr. Erwin W. Lutzer, "The Difference Between General and Special Revelations," *Moody Church Media*, https://www.moodymedia.org/articles/ difference-between-general-and-special-revelations/.

145 David Kinnaman, *You Lost Me. Why Young Christians are Leaving Church...* *and Rethinking Faith* (Grand Rapids, MI: BakerBooks, 2011), 132.

146 Tim Suttle, "Big, Juicy Questions," *Princeton Theological Seminary*, February 2, 2017, http://iym.ptsem.edu/big-juicy-questions/.

147 William Lane Craig, "The Kalam Cosmological Argument," *Reasonable Faith,* 2015, http://www.reasonablefaith.org/popular-articles-the-kalam-cosmological-argument.

148 William Lane Craig, "The Fine Tuning Argument," *Reasonable Faith,* http://www.reasonablefaith.org/transcript-fine-tuning-argument.

149 Ibid.

150 Rich Deem, "Quotes from Scientists Regarding Design of the Universe," *Evidence for God,* http://www.godandscience.org/apologetics/quotes.html#n04.

151 Lee Strobel, *The Case for Faith* (Grand Rapids, MI: Zondervan, 2000), 153.

152 Justin Taylor, "Is C.S. Lewis's Liar-Lord-or-Lunatic Argument Unsound?" *The Gospel Coalition,* February 1, 2016, https://blogs.thegospelcoalition.org/justintaylor/2016/02/01/is-c-s-lewiss-liar-lord-or-lunatic-argument-unsound/.

153 Ravi Zacharias, quoted in Josh McDowell, *New Evidence That Demands a Verdict* (Nashville: Thomas Nelson, 1999), 37-38.

154 Norman Geisler, quoted in Lee Strobel, *The Case for Faith* (Grand Rapids, MI: Zondervan, 2000), 131.

155 Dr. Gleason Archer cited in Josh McDowell, *New Evidence That Demands a Verdict* (Nashville: Thomas Nelson, 1999), 46.

156 Sir William Ramsay, quoted in Josh McDowell, *New Evidence That Demands a Verdict* (Nashville: Thomas Nelson, 1999), 61.

157 Josh McDowell, *The Last Christian Generation* (Holiday, FL: Green Key Books, 2006), 18.

158 Nancy Fitzgerald, *Anchorsaway Small Group Leader's Worldview Handbook* (Carmel, IN: Anchorsaway, 2006), 13.

159 Ibid, 22.

160 Dennis McCallum, "Five Worldviews", *Xenos Christian Fellowship,* http://www.xenos.org/essays/five-worldviews.

161 Jennifer Harper, "Eighty-four Percent of the World Population Has Faith; a Third are Christian," *The Washington Times,* December 23, 2012, http://www.washingtontimes.com/blog/watercooler/2012/dec/23/84-percent-world-population-has-faith-third-are-ch/.

162 David Papineau, "Naturalism ," *The Stanford Encyclopedia of Philosophy* (Winter 2016 Edition), Edward N. Zalta (ed.), https://plato.stanford.edu/archives/win2016/entries/naturalism/.

163 Phillip E. Johnson, *Darwin on Trial*.(Downers Grove, IL: InterVarsity Press, 2010), 220.

164 Nancy Fitzgerald, *Anchorsaway Small Group Leader's Worldview Handbook* (Carmel, IN: Anchorsaway, 2006), 14.

165 Ibid, 18.

166 Josh McDowell, *New Evidence That Demands a Verdict* (Nashville: Thomas Nelson, 1999), xlii.

167 Nancy Fitzgerald, *Anchorsaway Small Group Leader's Worldview Handbook*, (Carmel, IN: Anchorsaway, 2006), 16.

168 Josh McDowell and Sean McDowell, *The Unshakable Truth, How You Can Experience the Twelve Essentials of a Relevant Faith* (Eugene, OR: Harvest House Publishers, 2010), 23.

169 Christian Smith and Melinda Denton, quoted by Kenda Creasy Dean, *Almost Christian: What the Faith of Our Teenagers is Telling the American Church* (New York: Oxford University Press, 2010), 13.

170 Kenda Creasy Dean, *Almost Christian: What the Faith of Our Teenagers is Telling the American Church* (New York: Oxford University Press, 2010), 14.

171 "Ministry Overview," *Anchorsaway*, http://anchorsaway.org/about.

Conclusion

172 Francis Chan and Lisa Chan, *You and Me Forever: Marriage in Light of Eternity* (San Francisco: Claire Love Publishing, 2014), 117.

Morgan James
Speakers Group

↗ www.TheMorganJamesSpeakersGroup.com

We connect Morgan James published authors with live and online events and audiences who will benefit from their expertise.

CPSIA information can be obtained
at www.ICGtesting.com
Printed in the USA
LVOW03s2101280218
568205LV00004B/324/P